Country Cooking
Plain
and
Fancy

Country Cooking Plain and Fancy

Specialties of the House

Edited by
Elizabeth Hood

The Stephen Greene Press
Brattleboro, Vermont
Lexington, Massachusetts

The acknowledgments on pages 191–192 are also a part of this copyright page.

First Edition

Text copyright © 1983 by The Stephen Greene Press

This book is manufactured in the United States of America. It is designed by Kathleen Shulga and published by The Stephen Greene Press, Fessenden Road, Brattleboro, Vermont 05301.

Library of Congress Cataloging in Publication Data

Main entry under title:

Country cooking plain and fancy.

Includes index.
1. Cookery. I. Hood, Elizabeth, 1941–
TX715.C8613 1983   641.5   83–11618
ISBN 0–8289–0513–4 (pbk.)

Contents

Preface

Gathered here are recipes from twenty-seven cookbooks and as many and more experts. The collection is designed to stimulate your imagination, lift your spirits, and provide you with a quick answer to the perennial and maddening six o'clock question, "What's for dinner?"

Simple inexpensive dishes made with readily available ingredients is what country cooking is about. Some are plain, others, for special occasions, are fancy. Plain or fancy, these country dishes tend to become specialties of the house. You have your own. This collection will help you expand your repertoire and perhaps help you to find something different when you need it.

What you'll find here are classics prepared in a new way (Saurbraten using venison), old-time up-country recipes (deep-fried cucumbers), exotic dishes (Rolled Almond Cake from France) and humbler ones with a unique slant (Pizza Ratatouille). Each recipe is included because in one way or another it is unusual, refreshing, or just plain good. Standard recipes (New England Clam Chowder or Tuna-Noodle Casserole) are not included, nor are those which rely on convenience foods. The emphasis is on fresh, pure ingredients.

So what you have here is this inveterate browser's pick of favorites to be used year round or seasonally (when the fiddleheads are in), when hot hors d'oeuvres are the order of the day, or when a new dessert is called for.

All of the books from which these recipes were taken have been published by The Stephen Greene Press in Brattleboro, Vermont, with the exception of THE NATURAL WORLD COOKBOOK by Joe Freitus, which was published by Stonewall Press, and was, at the time this cookbook was being put together, distributed by The Stephen Greene Press. That cookbook is now available from Stackpole Books, Box 1831, Harrisburg, Pennsylvania 17105.

THE VENISON BOOK by Audrey Alley Gorton, from which two recipes have been taken, was published in 1957, one of the first books issued by a fledgling press. It is still in print. A number of recipes come from The Harvest Home Cookbook Series, a group of small specialty cookbooks. Some come from the classic on food preservation, PUTTING FOOD BY by Ruth Hertzberg, Beatrice Vaughan and Janet Greene, now out in its third edition. Many are from Beatrice Vaughan's various works, including THE OLD COOK'S ALMANAC, YANKEE HILL-COUNTRY COOKING and THE LADIES AID COOKBOOK. There are unusual soups from SOUP AND BREAD by Julia Older and Steve Sherman, a touch of France from Denise Khaitman Schorr's MY FRENCH KITCHEN, some gems from Camille Stagg's THE COOK'S ADVISOR, and more.

COUNTRY COOKING PLAIN AND FANCY is a collection of recipes that caught my eye. Savor them for what they bring to your table as they become specialties of the house.

Betsy Hood

Full references for the cookbooks begin on page 191.

Appetizers

Use any sprout available; alfalfa is most common.

Avocado-Cucumber Slices

⅔ cup sprouts (alfalfa, pea, bean, wheat, cabbage, radish)
1 medium-size cucumber
1 small avocado
1 or 2 cherry tomatoes
1 tablespoon lemon juice
1 teaspoon minced chives
salt and pepper to taste
small amount of wheat germ

Remove small slice from each end of cucumber, and lightly score the skin lengthwise. With melon baller or small scoop remove seeds and some of the cucumber pulp. Discard.

In a small bowl mash the avocado and beat with a fork until creamy. Add finely chopped sprouts and chopped tomatoes, lemon juice, chives, salt and pepper. If the mixture is too wet, add a little wheat germ. Mix thoroughly and pack into hollow cucumber.

Refrigerate for several hours and then slice crosswise with a very sharp knife. Arrange for serving alternately with any dark crisp crackers.

Serves 2–4   SPROUTS TO GROW AND EAT
Esther Munroe

From an antique 'receipt.'

Cucumbers in Batter

2 medium cucumbers, peeled
2 egg yolks, beaten
½ cup milk
¾ cup sifted flour
½ teaspoon salt
fat for frying

Cut cucumbers in ⅛-inch slices and cover with cold water. Let stand about 30 minutes. Drain, then dry on a paper towel.

Beat egg yolks until light, beating in milk, then the flour sifted in with the salt. Beat all well with rotary beater.

Dip each cucumber slice quickly into the batter and drop in deep, hot fat (390° F). Fry until brown and crisp on each side. Drain on paper and sprinkle with salt very lightly. Serve at once.

Enough for 6   THE OLD COOK'S ALMANAC
                                    Beatrice Vaughan

These two bean dips go well with crudités.

South of the Border

1 (15½-ounce) can red kidney beans (drained)
½ teaspoon chili powder (or more to taste)
½ teaspoon salt or garlic salt
1 clove garlic, minced (only if garlic salt is not used)
¼ cup finely chopped green pepper
1 (8-ounce) package cream cheese, softened

Mix in blender or with electric mixer until creamy. Can be served warmed or cold.

Makes about 2 cups   HORS D'OEUVRES BOOK
Marjorie Hamilton

Garbanzo Bean (Chickpea) Spread/Dip

2 cups well-cooked garbanzo beans
juice of 1–2 lemons
2–3 cloves garlic
2–3 tablespoons sesame butter (tahini)
1–3 teaspoons soy sauce (tamari) (optional — or small amount of salt)

Put a small amount of beans, plus the garlic cloves, in blender. (Too much at once does not make a smooth mix.) Add the other ingredients. Use the juice from cooking the beans for thinning the mixture. Taste as you go and adjust seasonings.

Makes about 2 cups   YOUR HEALTH UNDER SIEGE
Jeffrey Bland

Serve with crisp crackers.

Brandied Cheese Crock

½ pound shredded sharp cheese (Cheddar, Herkimer, Pro-
   volone, etc.), at room temperature
2 tablespoons softened butter or margarine
Dash hot pepper sauce
3–4 tablespoons brandy, to taste
3–4 tablespoons cream or Neufchatel cheese

Blend ingredients (using 3 tablespoons cream cheese) in food
processor or blender until smooth. Gradually add enough remaining cream cheese to make mixture very smooth and spread-
able. Pack into crock, cover, and refrigerate at least 1 day to
allow flavors to blend. Keeps for weeks and may be added to
whenever you have more dried cheese. Serve at room temperature.

Makes about 1 cup   THE COOK'S ADVISOR
                                         Camille J. Stagg

Variations: Crumble blue-veined cheeses and blend with Swiss or Emmenthaler
flavored with mustard. Bland, soft cheeses are compatible when blended with
another stronger favorite.

Hot and delightfully crunchy.

Stuffed Mushrooms

½ cup wheat, bean or alfalfa sprouts
8–10 large, fresh mushrooms
1 tablespoon finely minced onion
1 raw egg yolk
¼ cup grated cheese
1 tablespoon wheat germ
salt, pepper, and celery salt to taste

Wash and stem the mushrooms, reserving stems for use in another dish. Chop the sprouts very fine and add remaining ingredients. Mix well and stuff hollow side of mushrooms with sprout mixture. Broil for about 8 minutes and serve piping hot.

Serves 2–4
SPROUTS TO GROW AND EAT
Esther Munroe

Try this as an appetizer with pita bread.

Eggplant Relish

1 medium eggplant (about ½ pound)
1 clove garlic, minced
1 medium onion, chopped
1–2 medium tomatoes, chopped
⅓ cup chopped Greek or Italian olives
1 large green onion, chopped
about ⅓ cup minced parsley
about 1 tablespoon each: olive oil
    and lemon juice
salt and pepper to taste
lettuce
lemon slices
fresh mint sprigs

Bake eggplant in 350° F oven 40 to 50 minutes, until it is very soft and can be pierced easily with a fork. Let cool slightly, peel and chop coarse. Drain, pressing slightly to extract excess liquid. Place in bowl. Add ingredients through parsley. Gradually add equal parts oil and lemon juice to moisten. Toss to coat all ingredients. Season to taste. Adjust amount of oil, lemon juice, or seasoning. Cover and chill several hours or overnight. Serve over lettuce. Garnish with lemon slices and mint.

(Eggplant can be cooked in a microwave. Pierce in several places with sharp knife; place on paper toweling. Cook on high power 5 to 7 minutes, turning halfway through cooking for soft eggplant — longer for a firm one.)

Serves 4 as a salad   THE COOK'S ADVISOR
Camille J. Stagg

Prepare ahead and pop in the broiler at the last minute.

Bacon and Water Chestnuts

8 bacon strips
1 (10 ½-ounce) can whole water chestnuts
¼ cup soy sauce
¼ cup molasses

Cut bacon in thirds and wrap each piece around one water chestnut, securing with pick. Combine soy sauce and molasses and marinate bacon-wrapped chestnuts for a few hours.

Drain and place on broiler rack; bake at 375° F or about 20 minutes, or until bacon is crisp.

Yields about 24 rolls   HORS D'OEUVRES BOOK
Marjorie Hamilton

Delicious French cheese concoctions. To serve as an appetizer, use the large triangles of Gruyère, packaged 6 to a box, whole; to serve as an hors d'oeuvre, slice the large triangles in half or use the smaller ones, packaged 8 or 12 to the box.

Deep-Fried Cheese Triangles
(Friands au Fromage)

2 whole eggs
about 5 tablespoons breadcrumbs
1 box processed Gruyère cheese
1–1½ quarts salad oil or vegetable shortening (use enough to cover the bottom of your pan about 1 inch deep)

Break eggs into a small bowl and mix briskly with a fork. Spread breadcrumbs in a shallow dish. Slice the cheese triangles in half if serving as an hors d'oeuvre.

Dip each triangle of cheese first into the egg, then into the bread crumbs; coat well. Repeat dipping process once more.

To make the cheese bits easier to handle when frying, refrigerate for at least 1 hour (overnight if possible). Place on a cookie sheet or any adequate plate, stick toothpicks in each so that wrap will not adhere, cover with storage paper. Up to this point they can be prepared a day or two in advance.

Just before you are ready to serve, heat oil over medium heat for 10 minutes. If you are using an electric frying pan, 350° F should be the right temperature. If you use a frying thermometer, it should read between 360° F and 380° F.

Carefully drop cheese bits into oil and fry, 3 minutes on one side, 2 minutes on the other; or until golden brown. Don't crowd your pan; it's better to fry a few at a time.

Lift from oil and drain on crumpled paper towels on a cookie sheet.

To keep them warm, place them on a cookie sheet in a very slow oven until ready to serve. Unlike most fried foods, these delicacies will keep crisp for about 2 hours in a slow oven. Make sure the oven is at its lowest temperature.

Yields 6–12 cheese bits   MY FRENCH KITCHEN
                                             Denise Khaitman Schorr

Minced scallions and grated fresh ginger add interest to the filling; the steaming produces an unusual flavor and texture. Quite simple to prepare.

Steamed Buns Filled with Pork
(Cha Siew Bao)

Buns

1 tablespoon yeast
½ cup warm water
¼ teaspoon salt
1 cup unbleached all-purpose flour

Filling

½ pound ground mild pork sausage (or ground pork)
3 scallions, minced
½ teaspoon fresh ginger, grated
peanut oil

Dissolve yeast in water. Stir in salt. Mix in flour. Knead 5 minutes or until smooth and elastic. Cover. Let rise one hour.

Sauté scallions and ginger in peanut oil. Add meat and brown well. Mash up into small pieces. Set aside.

Punch down dough. Break off small egg-size pieces and pat flat into 3-inch circles. Place a tablespoon of pork mixture in center of each circle. Bring two opposite edges over and seal. With a knife cut off excess dough from remaining sides, leaving enough to seal in pork. Gently seal sides, tuck under along seam, and form miniature loaves. Cover and let rise for 15–20 minutes. Over boiling water place buns well apart in steamer basket to allow for expansion. Cover with lid. Steam for 5–10 minutes or until surface glistens and is firm to the touch. Serve warm.

Makes 10–12 SOUP AND BREAD
Julia Older and Steve Sherman

Bits of chopped olive and parsley add color and texture to this pâté.

Molded Liver Pâté

1 envelope unflavored gelatin
1 (10½-ounce) can condensed beef broth
½ teaspoon hot pepper sauce
2 (4¾-ounce) cans liver spread
1 cup sour cream
2 tablespoons minced onion
2 tablespoons fresh parsley, chopped
½ cup black olives, chopped fine
1 egg, hard-cooked

Dissolve gelatin in half the undiluted beef broth in a saucepan over low heat — about 4–5 minutes. Remove from heat and stir in remaining broth and hot sauce.

Mash liver with sour cream until smooth and add to the gelatin broth with the onion, parsley, and olives. Pour in lightly greased 4-cup mold and chill.

Unmold and decorate with sieved hard-cooked egg.

Makes one 4-cup mold HORS D'OEUVRES BOOK
Marjorie Hamilton

Chinese favorites. Make ahead and freeze or refrigerate until ready to use; oven heat before serving. Shrimp, chicken or pork are particularly nice in the filling. Beaten egg white brushed on edges before sealing will help them hold together.

Egg Rolls

Wrapping

> 2 eggs, well beaten
> 1½ cups water
> 2 cups flour
> ½ teaspoon salt
> oil for frying

Filling

> 2 cups Mung bean sprouts
> 1 cup cabbage, shredded fine
> 1 cup celery, shredded fine
> ¼ cup diced mushrooms
> 1 large onion, shredded fine
> 2 tablespoons soy sauce
> 2 cups leftover meat, shredded (optional)

For wrapping, combine all ingredients except oil. Heat 6-inch frying pan and grease lightly. Put one large spoonful of wrapping mixture in pan. Cook quickly without turning until bottom is brown and top is dry. Remove to plate. Repeat until all wrapping mix is used.

Combine all ingredients for filling in large bowl. Put about 2 tablespoons of filling mixture on each wrapping. Fold in sides and roll tightly. Deep fry until golden brown.

Yields about 15–18 rolls   SPROUTS TO GROW AND EAT
                                                Esther Munroe

An oyster tucked into a pastry 'purse' and oven-browned makes a delectable appetizer. A 19th century New England hill-country favorite.

Oyster Purses

10 large oysters
oyster liquid and milk
1 tablespoon melted butter or margarine
2 teaspoons flour
1 teaspoon salt
pinch of pepper
pastry for 1-crust pie

Drain oysters, reserving liquid. Measure and add enough milk to make ⅔ cup. Stir flour into melted butter, then stir into milk mixture. Cook over low heat, stirring constantly, until smooth and thick. Add ½ teaspoon of the salt and all the pepper. Sprinkle remaining salt over the oysters.

Roll pie pastry out to about ⅛ inch thick. Cut in 10 4-inch circles. Use trimmings to make 10 little strips about 3 × ¼ inches. Dip each oyster in sauce, coating each side. Place in the center of each circle, gathering pastry up to the center of the top as with the top of a bag. Press gently together and place a strip of pastry around, so the finished purse will look like a small bag gathered with a drawstring. Place each purse lightly on a buttered pan, flattening bottoms slightly. Bake in a 425° F oven for about 20 minutes or until brown and flaky. Serve hot.

THE OLD COOK'S ALMANAC
Beatrice Vaughan

An elegant and piquant first course. It should be prepared a day ahead.

Flounder Fillets with Mushrooms

1½ pounds flounder fillets
⅓ cup lime juice
⅓ cup flour
1 teaspoon salt
¼ teaspoon freshly ground pepper
¼ cup oil
1 cup chopped onion
½ pound mushrooms, sliced
1 clove garlic, crushed
1 bay leaf
1 cup white vinegar
lemon and lime wedges

Soak fillets in lime juice for 10 minutes. Dip in seasoned flour. Heat oil in a heavy skillet and cook fish quickly on both sides until lightly browned. Place fish in shallow dish.

Sauté the onion in the oil. Add mushrooms and cook 3 more minutes. Add garlic, bay leaf, and vinegar and bring to a boil. Pour over the fish. Cool.

Cover and chill overnight. Serve with lemon and lime wedges.

Serves 6
FISH COOKERY
James Vilkitis and Susan Uhlinger

Soups

Fruit soups are served in Scandinavia as a dessert, in Germany as a first course. Omit the whipped cream when serving as an appetizer and present smaller portions.

Fruit Soup (Cold)

½ cup raisins
½ cup prunes, cooked, pitted, and chopped
½ cup dried apricots, chopped
1 cup dry red wine
2 cups cold water
1 pound can tart pitted cherries with juice
2 tart cooking apples, peeled and diced
1 cinnamon stick
⅓ cup sugar
½ teaspoon grated orange or lemon rind
4 teaspoons arrowroot (2 tablespoons cornstarch may be substituted)
½ cup cold water
sugar to taste
Garnish: ½ cup heavy cream, whipped with 1 teaspoon confectioners' sugar

Soak dried fruit in red wine and water for 1 hour.

Place all fruit in heavy saucepan with the liquid. Add cinnamon stick and sugar and boil 15 minutes (or until apples are soft but not mushy). Mix arrowroot with ½ cup cold water and add this mixture to the soup. If soup is too tart, add more sugar. Add grated orange or lemon rind. Cook soup 2 minutes at slow boil.

Chill soup thoroughly. (May be put in freezer compartment until chilled to speed up process.)

Serve in chilled glass bowls or compotes with dollops of whipped cream and a sprinkle of nutmeg, cinnamon, and grated orange or lemon rind.

Serves 6–8   SOUP AND BREAD
Julia Older and Steve Sherman

Quick to prepare, this delicious cold soup topped with nasturtium or squash blossoms is a colorful prelude for a summer dinner.

Avocado Soup (Cold)

1½ cups avocado
2½ cups chicken stock (more for a thinner consistency)
2 teaspoons lemon juice
⅛ teaspoon Tabasco sauce
1 teaspoon grated onion
salt
Garnish: yellow nasturtium (or squash) blossoms

Halve avocado(s) and scoop out pulp. Place all ingredients with avocado in blender. Purée well. Chill soup thoroughly in blender container. Serve in chilled white or clear glass bowls.

Serves 4   SOUP AND BREAD
Julia Older and Steve Sherman

Spiced with chilis, this is a warming treat for a cold winter's day. A green salad and fresh bread are good accompaniments.

Black Bean Soup

1 cup black beans
⅛ pound salt pork, blanched
2 cups chicken stock
1 ripe medium-size tomato, diced
4 cups cold water
2 cloves garlic, crushed and minced
½ cup diced onion
¼ teaspoon hot pepper (dried, jalapēno sauce, or preserved whole chilis)
½ teaspoon oregano
1½ tablespoons olive oil
salt and pepper
2 tablespoons dry sherry
Garnish: sour cream

Wash and presoak beans 2–3 hours. To blanch salt pork, cover it with boiling water and let stand a few minutes.

Place beans, salt pork, chicken stock, tomato, and cold water in large soup pot. Bring to boil. Reduce heat and cover. Cook at slow boil for 1½–2 hours.

Sauté garlic, onion, red pepper or chili, and oregano in olive oil until onion is golden. Add mixture to beans. Salt and pepper soup to taste. Reserve 1 cup whole cooked beans. Purée remaining soup in blender.

Reheat *all* ingredients together 5 minutes. Stir in sherry. Ladle into bowls and float a dollop of sour cream in each.

Serves 4–6   SOUP AND BREAD
                                    Julia Older and Steve Sherman

An unusual and tasty soup topped with toasted sesame seeds. Stir tahini (available in health food stores) well before adding slowly to stock. This prevents curdling.

Broccoli-Tahini Soup

2 heaping cups broccoli flowers
water to cover and 2 tablespoons lemon juice
3 cups chicken stock
1 cup water
3 tablespoons sesame tahini
1 teaspoon lemon juice
salt to taste
Garnish: toasted sesame seeds

Cut broccoli flowers from stems. Cover flowers with cold water and 2 tablespoons lemon juice. Weight down with plate. Soak.

Drain broccoli and place in soup pot with chicken stock and 1 cup water. Bring broccoli to a boil. Lower heat and boil slowly, covered, until flowers are bright green but tender. Pour off 2 cups of the liquid. Cool and place in blender with tahini. (Or beat a little liquid at a time into the tahini with a whisk.) Blend.

Return tahini mixture to pot. Add 1 teaspoon lemon juice and salt to taste. Reheat and serve at once.

Serves 4   SOUP AND BREAD
Julia Older and Steve Sherman

New England bay scallops are best for this; cut up the larger variety. A pleasant contrast in texture is provided by the corn and the sweet pepper garnish.

Corn-Scallop Chowder

4 cups water
1 pound scallops
2 tablespoons sweet butter
1 cup diced onions
½ cup diced celery
1 tablespoon flour
1 cup diced potatoes
1 bay leaf
salt and white pepper to taste
2 cups milk
½ cup sour cream
1 cup kernel corn, drained
Garnish: minced sweet pepper

Bring water to boil. If using large sea scallops, cut into bite-size pieces. Add scallops to water and simmer for 5 minutes. Strain the liquid (reserve) and retain scallops in a bowl. Return scallop liquid to the heat and reduce by boiling to 2 cups.

Melt butter in a large heavy pot or frying pan. Sauté onions and celery in butter. Stir in flour. Add scallop liquid, ½ cup cooked scallops, potatoes, bay leaf, salt and white pepper. Simmer, covered, until potatoes are tender. Remove bay leaf.

Heat milk separately until tepid and whisk in sour cream. (Note: If milk gets too hot, sour cream will curdle.) Add this milk mixture to the soup pot along with remaining scallops and corn. Taste chowder again for salt and pepper.

Serves 4   SOUP AND BREAD
                                        Julia Older and Steve Sherman

A hearty, interesting fish soup. Try it with an unusual bread and a green salad.

Greek Lemon-Fish Soup

2 cups mild-flavored fish chunks
2 quarts water
1 cup diced potatoes
1 cup sliced carrots
½ cup diced celery
1 small onion, sliced
½ teaspoon dill
2 bay leaves
½ teaspoon salt
¼ teaspoon pepper
juice of 2 lemons
2 cups cooked rice or barley
¼ cup butter
lemon wedges

Simmer fish in 2 quarts water for 6 minutes. Remove fish and set aside. Add vegetables and seasonings to stock; simmer 1 hour.

Add rice or barley and lemon juice; heat. Heat fish chunks in melted butter, add to soup, and serve with lemon wedges.

Serves 8–10
FISH COOKERY
James Vilkitis and Susan Uhlinger

Lemon juice and cumin lighten the heaviness of lentils; the sausages and a garnish of thin lemon slices contrast nicely.

Lentil Lemon Soup

1½ cups lentils, washed
6   cups water
2   cups chicken or beef stock
1   potato (large) cut into 1-inch pieces
1   pound swiss chard (if unavailable, spinach)
⅓   cup minced onion
3   cloves garlic
4   tablespoons olive oil
2   tablespoons fresh minced celery leaves
¼   teaspoon coriander
salt and freshly ground pepper
3   tablespoons lemon juice
½   teaspoon cumin
link pork sausages (2 per person)
Garnish: thin lemon slices

Place lentils, water, and stock in soup pot and bring to a boil. (A soup bone may be added for extra flavor.) Turn heat to medium. Wash and drain chard. Take out the central white stem and slice layers of leaves into thin shreds. (Other greens may be substituted.) Add greens and potatoes. Slowly boil the soup, covered, for 45 minutes.

Crush garlic cloves first to enhance flavor, then mince with onion. Add to hot olive oil in a small frying pan. Sauté until tender. Add celery leaves and coriander. Add onion mixture to soup.

Brown sausages while the soup simmers another 5 minutes. (If sausages are not precooked, start them with the onions.)

Stir in salt, pepper, lemon juice, and cumin at the last minute. Serve in deep pottery bowls with 2 link sausages cut up into each serving.

Serves 6   Soup and Bread
                          Julia Older and Steve Sherman

A nutritious meatless soup.

Manybean Soup

1 onion, chopped
¼ cup oil
1½ teaspoons paprika
1 cup pinto beans
8–10 cups of water or vegetable stock
1 bay leaf
1 cup kidney beans
1 cup lima beans
1 cup yellow split peas
1½ teaspoons dillweed
4 teaspoons salt
¼ teaspoon pepper
1 tablespoon celery seed
Optional: chopped vegetables

Sauté onion lightly in oil, with paprika.

Rinse beans and peas in cold water and add them to the onion along with the water or stock, celery seed, bay leaf, and other spices. Partially cover the pot and cook for about 1 hour.

Makes about 8–9 cups   Your Health Under Siege
                          Jeffrey Bland

A handsome way to start a dinner party, this unique soup provides plenty of leeway for creative design. Lobster or shrimp may be substituted for the chicken; bamboo shoots may be used instead of water chestnuts.

Molded Chinese Soup

1 large chicken breast, split
1 dried Chinese mushroom (soaked in ½ cup water)
6 ounces cooked thin ham, sliced in ¼-inch wide strips
4 ounces sliced water chestnuts
3 slices gingerroot (¼-inch thick)
2 green onions (stems and all) cut into 1-inch pieces
sesame or peanut oil
2 eggs, slightly beaten
8–10 whole snow peas
4½ cups chicken stock
soy sauce to taste
Garnish: alfalfa sprouts

Steam chicken breast in a steamer 7–10 minutes. Tear meat off chicken into shreds.

Soak dried mushroom in warm water and remove stem. Rinse. Drain.

Prepare ham, water chestnuts, ginger, green onions. Refrigerate all meats and vegetables until ready for use.

In an 8-inch frying pan coated with oil, make 2 very thin omelets one at a time. Slice into long ½-inch strips.

In bowl with a bottom at least 6–8 inches in diameter, center mushroom, smooth side down. Arrange chicken, ham, and egg strips alternately spiraling from sides of mushroom. (Ingredients may be layered up sides of bowl, too). Fill in with snow peas and green onions. Place water chestnut strips at center of wheel.

Press ingredients down tightly with palm of your hand or a spatula. Cover them with ½ cup stock and sprinkle with soy sauce.

Place bowl in steamer, or large covered wok. Fill steamer bottom with approximately 2 inches of water and place bowl of vegetables and meats on a trivet in the bottom. Cover. Steam 20 minutes.

In separate pan heat chicken stock to slow boil. Select a serving bowl that will hold the steamed vegetable bowl, or use your wok. Invert steamed vegetable bowl in the bottom of the serving bowl (as you would to turn out an upside-down cake). But don't remove the bowl-mold. Instead, pour the stock around the inverted bowl. The suction of the liquid around the mold will release any vegetables that might stick to the bottom of the mold.

Now, pry up the molded vegetable bowl with two spoons and carefully lift it off. The Chinese vegetables and meats will float in a circular molded shape in the stock. Serve immediately at the table from the large serving bowl.

Serves 4   SOUP AND BREAD
                                  Julia Older and Steve Sherman

An old New England 'receipt' for the first garden peas. The recipe calls for young, tender peas and the pods are used as well in the cooking. The result is wonderful.

Creamy Green Pea Soup

2   pounds fresh green peas, unshelled
1   large onion, cut up
6   cups water
1   teaspoon salt
pinch of pepper
2   tablespoons melted butter
2   tablespoons flour
1½ cups milk
½   cup light cream

Select peas whose pods are fresh and green. Shell, saving pods. Wash pods well, then simmer them with the water and the onion for about 45 minutes. Drain, reserving liquid and discarding pods.

Return the liquid to heat, add peas, salt, and pepper. Simmer until peas are very tender. With strainer spoon, remove about ⅔ cup peas and reserve.

The remainder, liquid and all, put through a sieve. Mix flour with the melted butter, then stir in the liquid mixture. Cook over low heat until smooth and thickened, stirring constantly. Add reserved peas, the milk and the cream. Heat very hot but *don't* boil. Add more salt, if desired.

Serves 6–8   THE OLD COOK'S ALMANAC
                                          Beatrice Vaughan

Short ribs do double duty here. After the stock is made, the ribs are crisped and browned in the oven and served alongside the soup. Use any fresh vegetables; avoid tired leftovers, they spoil the texture.

Vegetable-Short Rib Soup

5 cups water
½ cup diced onion
1 bay leaf
1 tablespoon minced fresh celery leaves
2 pounds short ribs, cut into 3-inch pieces
¼ cup barley
¾ cup diced potato
¾ cup diced carrot
¾ cup diced celery
1 cup chopped cabbage
1 cup fresh whole peeled tomatoes
salt and freshly ground black pepper to taste
Garnish: minced chives

Bring water, onion, bay leaf, and celery leaves to a boil in wide-bottomed soup pot. Add short ribs. Lower heat and boil slowly 1½ hours.

Remove meat. The meat will leave a fat layer floating on top. Degrease the soup with a large spoon. Add barley to soup and cook covered at slow boil ½ hour. Add vegetables, salt and pepper. Cover, and boil slowly 20 minutes.

Place meat in shallow baking dish and put it in the oven to crisp and brown at 350° F while vegetables cook. Serve short ribs in separate dish at the table.

Serves 6–8

SOUP AND BREAD
Julia Older and Steve Sherman

Rich and elegant, smooth and creamy, this makes a fitting first course for special guests.

Scallop Soup, St. Jacques

½ cup dry white wine
½ cup water
4 peppercorns
1 bay leaf
1 sprig parsley
2 tablespoons minced shallots
1 cup chicken broth
¾ pound sea scallops
2 tablespoons sweet butter
1 tablespoon flour
1 cup light cream
¼ cup grated Parmesan cheese
¼ cup grated Gruyère cheese
1 egg yolk
salt and cayenne to taste
Garnish: fresh minced parsley

Place wine, water, peppercorns, bay leaf, parsley, shallots, and chicken broth in a saucepan and bring to a boil. Lower heat and add scallops (cut into bite size). Boil them gently in this liquid for approximately 10 minutes, or until they are tender. Strain the broth into a bowl. Save the scallops and shallots but discard parsley, peppercorns, and bay leaf.

Melt butter in a small saucepan and stir in flour with a whisk. Add light cream and cheese. As soon as this mixture thickens, remove from heat and stir in the scallop broth. Place egg yolk, scallops, shallots, and 2 cups of the liquid in a blender or run through a food mill. Purée well. Return all ingredients to a large soup pan and heat. Do not boil. Serve in small portions garnished with minced parsley.

Serves 4   SOUP AND BREAD
                                           Julia Older and Steve Sherman

Meats

The meat is tenderized by the spicy marinade and slow, moist cooking.

Sliced Texas Steak with Barbeque Sauce

3 pounds round steak, cut 1-inch thick
¾ cup sliced onion
⅓ cup red wine vinegar
¼ cup salad oil
1 clove garlic, sliced
1 teaspoon Worcestershire sauce
1 teaspoon salt
1 teaspoon chili powder
½ teaspoon dry mustard
¼ teaspoon pepper
1 tablespoon shortening
1 (8-ounce) can tomato sauce
¼ cup brown sugar, firmly packed
½ lemon, thinly sliced

Place the steak in a shallow dish or plastic bag. Combine the onion, vinegar, oil, garlic, Worcestershire sauce, salt, chili powder, mustard and pepper and pour over the steak. Refrigerate all together 8 to 10 hours, or overnight, turning several times.

Remove the steak from the marinade, saving the marinade. Heat the shortening in a heavy skillet; add the meat and brown well on both sides. Separate the sliced onion from the marinade and add to the browned steak with ⅓ cup of the marinade mixture. Cover the steak and cook slowly until it is fork tender, about 2 hours.

Remove the meat from the pan; skim off the excess fat and keep hot. Add the remaining marinade, tomato sauce, brown sugar and lemon to the pan drippings. Simmer about 15 minutes to blend the flavors. Slice the meat very thin, diagonally, across the grain and serve with the sauce.

Serves 8   STEAK COOKBOOK
                              Jean H. Shepard

Prepared the day before, this is a piquant loaf to serve with potato salad on a sultry summer day.

Spiced Beef

2 pounds stewing beef, cut up
1 beef soup-bone
1½ teaspoons salt
pinch of pepper
2 tablespoons vinegar
1 large onion, cut up
8 cups water
1 teaspoon sage
¼ teaspoon each thyme and mustard
pinch each red pepper and cloves
pinch each mace and ground allspice

Place first seven ingredients in soup kettle, cover and simmer until meat is very tender, 2 to 3 hours.

Remove meat and bone from broth. Strain broth, add spices and simmer uncovered until broth is reduced to about 2 cups. Chop beef rather fine, add to broth and mix well. Pour into standard size bread tin and chill in refrigerator overnight. Slice to serve.

Serves 8–10   THE OLD COOK'S ALMANAC
                             Beatrice Vaughan

Strips of marinated beef, sprouts, scallions, mushrooms, and shredded snow peas combine beautifully in this quick and easy stir-fried dish.

Spiced Beef and Bean Sprouts

2 cups mung bean sprouts
1 tablespoon vegetable oil
1 tablespoon soy sauce
¼ teaspoon Tabasco sauce
pinch of salt
pinch of powdered ginger
½ pound lean beefsteak (tenderloin or round)
2 tablespoons peanut, safflower, or corn oil
3 scallions, cut in short lengths
½ cup mushrooms, sliced thin
¾ cup snow peas, shredded
½ cup beef broth or bouillon
1 tablespoon cornstarch

In a shallow bowl combine vegetable oil, soy sauce, Tabasco sauce, salt and ginger. Cut beef into 1-inch wide strips and slice very thin across the grain. Put sliced beef in the soy sauce marinade, let sit for one hour and drain.

Heat the 2 tablespoons of peanut, safflower or corn oil in wok or heavy frying pan. Stir-fry the drained meat for 2 minutes and remove from pan.

Put scallions, mushrooms and snow peas in the pan. Stir-fry for 1 or 2 minutes. Add sprouts and stir-fry for 3 or 4 minutes. Add partially cooked meat and cook, covered, for another 3 or 4 minutes.

Meanwhile combine the beef broth or bouillon and cornstarch. Add to the meat-sprouts mixture and blend well, cooking another 1 or 2 minutes. Serve with noodles or rice.

Serves 2–4   SPROUTS TO GROW AND EAT
                                  Esther Munroe

This elegant barbequed steak has a melted blue cheese-and-chives topping.

Marinated Flank Steak

½ cup salad oil
¼ cup lemon juice
1 tablespoon grated onion
2 tablespoons chopped parsley
1 teaspoon dried leaf marjoram
1 teaspoon dried leaf thyme
1 teaspoon salt
1 clove garlic, minced
½ teaspoon Tabasco pepper sauce
¼ cup butter or margarine
2 tablespoons chopped chives
2 tablespoons blue cheese
1½ pounds flank steak, scored

In a small jar, combine the salad oil and lemon juice. Add the onion, parsley, marjoram, thyme, salt, garlic, and Tabasco sauce; cover and shake to mix thoroughly. Place the steak in a shallow glass or enamel pan; pour the oil mixture over the steak; cover and marinate in the refrigerator for 2 hours. Meanwhile, cream the butter with the chives and blue cheese; set aside.

Prepare a charcoal fire. When it reaches the light grey ash stage (or red glow at night), remove the flank steak from the marinade and place on the grill about 2 or 3 inches above the briquets. Brush the steak with marinade, and grill 5 minutes on each side. Remove the broiled steak to a carving board; spread with cheese-chive mixture; slice diagonally and serve immediately.

Serves 4–6

STEAK COOKBOOK
Jean H. Shepard

A vegetable and beef roll served with a tasty gravy.

South American Beef Steak Roll

2 pounds round steak, cut in a single ½-inch-thick piece
¼ cup red wine vinegar
1 clove garlic, minced
¼ teaspoon leaf thyme
¼ teaspoon pepper
1 small bay leaf
1 teaspoon salt
1 cup soft breadcrumbs
2 cups fresh spinach leaves
½ cup thinly sliced onion
4 slender carrots, about 8 inches long, left whole or quart-
      ered lengthwise
¼ cup chopped parsley
2 tablespoons shortening
1 (10½-ounce) can condensed beef broth, undiluted
¼ cup water
2 tablespoons flour

Place the meat in a large shallow baking dish. Combine and mix
the next five ingredients. Pour this mixture over meat; cover
and refrigerate 1 hour. Drain the meat, saving the marinade.
Sprinkle the salt on the meat and arrange a layer of breadcrumbs, spinach, onion and carrots in turn over the meat; sprinkle the parsley over all. Roll up and tie securely in several places.

Using a large frying pan, brown the steak roll well in hot shortening over moderate heat. Place the steak in a shallow 1½ quart baking dish, pouring the pan drippings, reserved marinade and broth over the top. Cover the dish with aluminum foil, crimping the edges to the rim of the dish, and bake in a moderate (350° F) oven until the meat is tender, 2 to 2½ hours. Remove the meat from the pan; keep warm.

To make the gravy, pour the drippings into a large measuring cup. Spoon off the excess fat and add water to make 1½ cups liquid. Mix the ¼ cup water and the flour until free of lumps; stir into the drippings. Cook all, stirring constantly, until the gravy is thickened. Then serve with the freshly sliced steak and vegetable roll.

Serves 6   STEAK COOKBOOK
                                           Jean H. Shepard

Overnight soaking in a marinade produces a pot roast with just a hint of sweetness. Delicious served hot with pan gravy and also excellent cold.

Lemon Pot Roast

1 (6-ounce) can frozen lemonade concentrate, thawed
⅔ cup apple juice
1 medium onion, sliced
2 bay leaves
1½ teaspoons salt
¼ teaspoon pepper
1 teaspoon cinnamon
½ teaspoon ground cloves
chuck pot roast of beef, 4–5 pounds
2 tablespoons melted fat
1 cup dairy sour cream

Combine first eight ingredients and pour over the meat, which has been placed in a large bowl. Cover and let stand in refrigerator overnight. Turn meat several times before cooking.

Remove meat from the marinade and brown in the melted fat. Remove meat to baking pan. Pour marinade into the frying pan and heat to boiling. Pour over the meat. Cover baking pan and bake about 3 hours in a 325° F oven, or until meat is tender. Remove meat to serving platter and stir sour cream into the pan juices. Heat very hot but don't boil. Serve pan gravy with the meat.

Serves 6

Citrus Cooking
Beatrice Vaughan

Good hot or cold, the pork is complemented nicely by orange sections, grated rind, and jelly.

Roast Pork with Oranges

pork roast, about 4 pounds
1 teaspoon ground sage
1½ teaspoons salt
pinch of pepper
1 cup water
2 tablespoons any jelly
grated rind of 1 large orange
juice of 2 large oranges
3 large oranges, peeled and sectioned

Rub pork with the sage, salt, and pepper. Place on a rack in a roasting pan and pour in the cup of water. Bake uncovered in a 350° F oven for 1½ hours.

With a large spoon, skim out fat in pan, leaving the meat juices. Combine jelly and grated orange rind. Spread over pork. Add orange juice. Bake until meat is very tender, about 1½ hours longer (if pan appears dry during that time, add a little hot water).

Add orange sections to pan juices and bake 5 minutes longer. Remove meat to serving platter. Serve oranges and the sauce as accompaniments to the pork.

Serves 6

Citrus Cooking
Beatrice Vaughan

A hearty, inexpensive all-in-one dish topped with stuffed olives and crumbled bacon.

Southwest Meat Pie

    4 large slices bacon
    1 pound hamburger
    1 cup drained whole-kernel corn
    ¼ cup finely chopped green pepper
    1 small onion, finely chopped
    ¼ cup cornmeal
    ½ teaspoon oregano
    ½ teaspoon chili powder
    1 teaspoon salt
small pinch of pepper
    1 (8-ounce) can tomato sauce
    1 egg
    ¼ cup milk
    ½ teaspoon dry mustard
    ½ teaspoon Worcestershire sauce
    1 cup shredded sharp cheese (¼ lb.)
    6 stuffed olives, sliced
unbaked 9-inch pie shell

Fry bacon until crisp, drain. Pour off the fat, then brown hamburger in the pan. Add vegetables, cornmeal, oregano, chili powder, salt, pepper and tomato sauce. Stir all well, pour mixture into the pie shell. Bake in a 425° F oven for 25 minutes; remove.

Beat together the egg and milk, mustard and Worcestershire sauce, and stir in the cheese. Spread over the top of the pie, then scatter sliced olives over all. Crumble the bacon and scatter

over olives. Return pie to the oven and bake 15 minutes longer,
or until cheese has melted. Remove from the oven and let stand
for 10 minutes before serving.

Serves 6   THE LADIES AID COOKBOOK
                                                Beatrice Vaughan

Top grade maple syrup is not needed for these sweet-sour oven-barbequed ribs.

Maple-Barbequed Spareribs

about 3 pounds spareribs
1 cup maple syrup
2 tablespoons chili sauce
2 tablespoons vinegar
1 small onion, peeled and minced
2 tablespoons Worcestershire sauce
1 teaspoon salt
½ teaspoon dry mustard
⅛ teaspoon pepper

Cut spareribs into serving-size pieces. Combine the remaining
ingredients and brush mixture on all sides of ribs. Arrange in
single layer in baking pan and bake in a 375° F oven until ribs
are very tender, 1½ to 2 hours. Brush meat with the sauce often
and turn pieces frequently so all portions will be coated with this
wonderful sauce.

Serves 4–6   REAL, OLD-TIME YANKEE MAPLE COOKING
                                                Beatrice Vaughan

Sauced with wine, the humble hamburger takes on new life.

Biftecks Miremonde

1½ slices stale bread, crumbled
4 tablespoons milk
1 onion, finely chopped
2 tablespoons butter, melted
¾ pound slightly fatty ground beef
2 eggs, beaten
1 tablespoon uncooked white cornmeal
salt and pepper
dash grated nutmeg
¼ cup white wine
1 teaspoon chopped parsley

Soak the crumbled stale bread in the milk. Sauté the chopped onion in the melted butter and add to the ground beef along with the soaked bread, beaten eggs, cornmeal, salt, pepper, and nutmeg. Mix all together well and let stand for 1 hour or more.

Shape the meat mixture into cakes about 1 inch thick and cook slowly in butter in a heavy skillet, covered, for about 10 minutes on each side. They should be brown and a little crusty on the outside but soft and light inside. When done, place the *Biftecks* on a hot platter. Add the wine and parsley to the butter remaining in the pan; heat, stir and boil 1 to 2 minutes. Pour the sauce over the *Biftecks* and serve.

Serves 4–5

STEAK COOKBOOK
Jean H. Shepard

Pork and apples marry beautifully in this hill-country recipe.

Cheshire Pork Pie with Apples

1 batch pie pastry for two crusts
2 pounds lean pork
4 medium apples
2 tablespoons white sugar
1 teaspoon salt
⅛ teaspoon pepper
¼ teaspoon ground sage
1 cup sweet cider
1 tablespoon butter
1 beaten egg

Cut pork in strips 1 × 2 inches. Peel and slice apples. Line a deep pie plate with pie dough rolled about ⅛ inch thick. Put in a layer of pork and sprinkle with a little of the salt, pepper, and sage. Next, add a layer of the apple slices with some of the sugar sprinkled over them. Continue making alternate layers of pork and apples until all are used. Add sweet cider and dot top layer with the butter.

Cover with the top crust, in which several slits have been made. Brush crust with beaten egg and bake in a 350° F oven for about 1 hour and 30 minutes.

Serves 6   YANKEE HILL-COUNTRY COOKING
                                  Beatrice Vaughan

Pork chops are marinated 24 hours. Well worth the wait when served with its rich, delectable, very French sauce.

Marinated Pork Chops Sautéed with a Tangy Sour Cream Sauce
Côtes de Porc Sauce Poivrade

Marinating the Chops

    4–6 rib pork chops, ¾ to 1 inch thick, weighing about ¼
        pound each
    salt and pepper
    ⅔ cup dry white wine
    ⅔ cup red wine vinegar
    2 bay leaves
    1 teaspoon dried thyme
    ¾ cup chopped onion (1 medium onion)
    ½ cup chopped raw carrot (1 medium carrot)
    1 teaspoon table salt
    ¼ teaspoon freshly ground black pepper, medium grind

Trim excess fat from chops. Sprinkle both sides with salt and pepper.

Using a dish large enough to spread chops in without crowding (8½ × 8½ × 1½ inches), combine marinade ingredients and stir well.

Plunge chops into marinade and cover well. Refrigerate for 24 hours, basting and turning several times.

Sautéing

    5 tablespoons clarified butter

When ready to cook, heat butter to sizzling in a skillet large enough to accommodate chops without crowding (a 10-inch pan). Rather than crowd them, do a few at a time.

Take chops from marinade and pat with paper towel to remove moisture. Sauté 5 to 6 minutes on each side over medium heat until golden brown.

Cover skillet and let simmer 15 minutes over low heat.

Transfer chops to serving platter, cover (if you don't have a fitted cover use aluminum foil), and keep warm either in a slow oven or on a hot tray.

Completing the Sauce

¾ cup hot bouillon, either chicken or beef (or use home-made stock)
3 tablespoons soured cream
1 teaspoon potato flour (all-purpose flour may be substituted)
2 tablespoons cold water
2 tablespoons chopped fresh parsley

Pour remaining butter from skillet and put in liquid from marinade. Boil over medium heat for 5 minutes, uncovered. Add hot bouillon.

Reduce this liquid over high heat for 3 to 5 minutes, stirring and scraping skillet with wooden spoon.

Spoon soured cream into a bowl. Add several tablespoons of liquid from skillet and whisk. Slowly add this mixture to skillet, whisking vigorously.

Measure potato flour into a cup or small bowl; add water one tablespoon at a time, stirring well. Stir several tablespoons of liquid from skillet into this mixture; then add mixture to skillet, whisking well. The flour will cause the sauce to thicken slightly and give it an appetizing lustre. Taste and correct seasoning if necessary.

Strain sauce over chops on platter; press vegetables to extract all juices.

Sprinkle with parsley. Serve at once.

Serves 4–6   MY FRENCH KITCHEN
                                                  Denise Khaitman Schorr

Traditionally served cold, a pork loin roasted and braised is a specialty of Perigord (where the best truffles are found). It is just as tasty served hot.

Braised Pork with Green Peppercorns, Garlic, and Herbs
(Enchaud)

4¼–4½-pound eye of the loin pork roast
lots of garlic (at least 7 large cloves)
1 heaping teaspoon green peppercorns
table salt
1 cup lukewarm water
8 tablespoons fresh chopped parsley
8 tablespoons fresh (or freeze-dried) chopped chives
8 tablespoons fresh (or freeze-dried) chopped chervil

Preheat oven to 400° F. Trim off and reserve excess fat from the roast. Pat with paper towels to absorb surface moisture. Peel and cut garlic into slivers. Starting at one end, cut three or four short slits across the width of the roast and insert garlic in them. Repeat procedure about every inch along the length of the meat. Turn and cut short slits down the length of the roast. Insert green peppercorns, about two or three every inch. Before inserting the green peppercorns, crush them lightly to release their flavor.

With a piece of fat from the roast, coat the bottom of a large roasting pan. Place pork in it, uncovered. Reduce oven temperature to 350° F and brown on all sides. (This should take about 45 minutes.) Sprinkle salt on each side of roast, add water, cover, and braise for 1 hour and 15 minutes. (If the cover is fitted with a vent, make sure it is closed.) Baste the meat with the pan gravy every 20 minutes, turning it so that it browns evenly.

While the roast is cooking, mix the parsley, chives, and chervil together. When the roast is done, transfer it to a platter and pour some of the pan gravy over it. Spread half the herb mixture down the length of the roast and carefully pour on more of the gravy to set the herb mixture. Turn roast on the other side and repeat with remaining gravy and herb mixture. Let the roast cool completely, for about 2 hours. Place toothpicks in the roast so the herbs won't be disturbed, cover with storage wrap, and refrigerate. When serving, leave at room temperature for ½ hour.

Remove toothpicks and present the whole roast before slicing it. The slices should be no thicker than ½ inch.

Serves 8   My French Kitchen
                                   Denise Khaitman Schorr

Homespun country cooking at its best.

Supper Pie

1 pound link sausages
2 medium onions, peeled and thinly sliced
2 medium apples, peeled and thinly sliced
1 tablespoon flour
1 chicken bouillon cube
1 cup boiling water
pinch of pepper
salt, if needed
2½ cups seasoned mashed potato
paprika

Cook sausages until brown; drain. Cut each link in 3 pieces and place in deep, 9-inch pie plate. Pour off all but 2 tablespoons of fat from frying pan. Add onions and apples and simmer in the pan until tender. Do not allow to brown. With a strainer spoon, remove onions and apples.

Blend the flour with fat remaining in the pan, then add the bouillon cube and boiling water, stirring constantly. Simmer until smooth and thick. Return onions and apples to sauce, add pepper and salt to taste. Pour all over the sausages, spread mashed potatoes over the top and sprinkle lightly with paprika. Bake in 350° F oven until browned, about 30 minutes. Serve hot.

Serves 4–6   REAL, OLD-TIME YANKEE APPLE COOKING
                                            Beatrice Vaughan

Sweet Italian sausages also work well in this recipe. Serve with chunks of warm Italian bread.

Sausages and Green Peppers

  2 pounds link sausages
10 sweet green peppers (medium)
  2 medium onions
     pinch of thyme
     pinch of sage
     pinch of oregano
     grated Parmesan cheese (optional)

Place sausages — do not prick them yet — in a heavy kettle and just barely cover with water; boil 15 minutes, then drain off and discard the water. Now, prick each sausage several times with a fork, allowing the fat to spurt into the kettle.

Seed each pepper and cut into quarters. Peel onions and cut into chunks. Arrange peppers and onions over the top of the sausages. Add the seasonings. Cover the kettle and set over a very low flame, just hot enough to keep the contents simmering. Stir occasionally and add a tiny bit of hot water if the mixture cooks dry. Cook about 45 minutes. Serve at once with the grated Parmesan sprinkled over each portion, if desired.

Serves 6   THE LADIES AID Cookbook
                                   Beatrice Vaughan

Sausage and apples were made for each other. Here are two examples of ways to combine them.

Stuffed Wild Apples

8–10 wild apples
1 pound ground sausage meat
½ pound breadcrumbs
cinnamon or nutmeg
salt to taste

Use large semi-ripe apples for best flavor. Wash and core but do not peel. Place the apples on a buttered baking pan. Mix the ground sausage meat and breadcrumbs. Stuff each cored apple, place in a 350° F oven and bake until tender. You might want to add a little salt for flavor. Serve hot, sprinkled with a little cinnamon.

Serves 4–5   THE NATURAL WORLD COOKBOOK
Joe Freitus

Apple Sausage Cakes

1 pound bulk sausage, as lean as possible
1 cup grated raw apple (about 2 medium)
⅔ cup soft breadcrumbs
1 egg, beaten

Combine sausage and apple; mix breadcrumbs with beaten egg, add to first mixture. Shape into 6 rather flat cakes. Start in cold frying pan and cook slowly for about 30 minutes. Turn often until brown on both sides. Pour off fat occasionally.

Serves 6   REAL, OLD-TIME YANKEE APPLE COOKING
Beatrice Vaughan

An old Pennsylvania Dutch recipe that makes for good eating.

Ham and Dried Apples with Egg Dumplings

end of ham with bone, about 3 pounds
2 cups dried apples
2 tablespoons light brown sugar

Soak dried apples for several hours (or overnight if they're quite leathery) until they've softened a bit and begun to plump. Meanwhile cover ham with cold water and bring to a boil, covered. Simmer about 2 hours, then add drained apples; simmer about 1 hour longer. Remove ham to a platter, lift apples from the pot with a slotted spoon, place them around the ham, and sprinkle with sugar. Keep all hot while the dumplings are cooking.

Serves 6

Egg Dumplings

1½ cups sifted flour
3 teaspoons baking powder
½ teaspoon salt
1 tablespoon butter or magarine
about ¼ cup milk
1 beaten egg

Sift flour with baking powder and salt. Rub in the butter with your fingertips and stir in enough milk to make a soft dough. Stir in the beaten egg.

Drop from a spoon into the boiling ham broth. Cover tightly and simmer about 12 minutes. Arrange dumplings on the platter around the ham and apples, and serve.

PUTTING FOOD BY
Ruth Hertzberg, Beatrice Vaughan, Janet Greene

*No fussing at the last minute with this recipe. With hot French bread,
a country feast fit for a king.*

Venison Pot Roast with Vegetables

3–4 pound pot roast
¼ cup salt pork, cubed small
2 tablespoons butter
6 carrots
6 small onions
6 small potatoes
1 stalk celery
1 teaspoon parsley flakes
¼ teaspoon thyme
1 cup dry white wine (or red, if you don't mind the pinkish
   tinge to the vegetables)
salt and pepper
1½ cups hot water

Lard the roast well by inserting the cubes of salt pork into crev-
ices in the meat. Heat butter in a Dutch oven or deep casserole
and brown the meat on all sides. Add the hot water, wine, carrots,
onions, celery, parsley, thyme and salt and pepper. Cover and
cook gently for 3 hours on top of the stove or in the oven, or
until the meat is tender. (Simmering is important: it keeps the
meat tender and juicy and prevents the vegetables from disin-
tegrating.) If the liquid gets too low, add water, or water and
wine in the proportion you started with.

About 30 minutes before the meal is to be served, add the
potatoes, peeled and halved, correcting the seasoning since the

potatoes tend to draw saltiness from the liquid. When the potatoes are done, remove the meat and vegetables, discarding the celery if it is bedraggled.

If necessary, reduce the liquid rapidly over high heat while keeping the pot roast and the vegetables hot. Arrange the meat and vegetables on a deep hot platter, pour some of the pot-liquor over the top, put the rest in a gravy boat, and serve.

Serves 6–8   THE VENISON BOOK
Audrey Alley Gorton

Don't be put off by the gingersnaps in the gravy. They add a certain something to this unusual venison recipe. Serve with noodles and Spicy Apple Cole Slaw (Page 127).

Sauerbraten

3–4 pound piece of venison (the neck may be used)
salt pork for larding
1 onion, peeled and sliced
1 clove garlic
¼ cup sugar
12 whole cloves
1 teaspoon peppercorns
1 tablespoon dry English mustard
salt
vinegar (tarragon is good) and water in equal parts to half
    cover the meat
1 cup sour cream
4 gingersnaps (maybe)
fat for frying

Lard the meat by threading it in several places with thin strips of salt pork drawn by a larding needle. If this seems too difficult you may omit the larding; it won't make too much difference.

Put the meat in an earthenware crock or bowl. Heat (do not boil) the vinegar and water, add the seasonings and pour over the meat. Cover and let stand from 4 to 8 days, turning the meat once or twice each day.

Remove the meat from the marinade, rub with garlic and dredge well with flour. Melt the fat in a Dutch oven or deep heavy saucepan with a tight-fitting cover. Brown the meat on all sides, pour the marinade over it, cover closely, and simmer over a low flame for 2 to 3 hours, or until tender.

When the meat is done remove it from the pan and keep it hot; thicken the gravy with flour mixed with water or wine to make a thin paste. Now is the time to add the gingersnaps if you can bring yourself to do it! Just before serving add the sour cream and pour the gravy over the meat.

Serves 6–8   THE VENISON BOOK
Audry Alley Gorton

Poultry
and
Fish

Sautéed chicken with a zesty cranberry-orange sauce.

Maritime Chicken

1 3-pound chicken (broiler-fryer), cut in pieces
½ cup flour
dash of salt
4 tablespoons butter
1½ cups cranberries
¼ cup chopped onion
1 teaspoon grated orange peel
¼ teaspoon ginger
¼ teaspoon cinnamon
¾ cup sugar
¾ cup orange juice

Shake chicken pieces in a bag with flour and dash of salt until covered. Brown chicken pieces in butter, turning once.

Combine remaining ingredients in a saucepan, and bring to a boil to make sauce. Pour sauce over chicken. Cover and cook slowly about 40 minutes.

Serves 4–6   THE CRANBERRY CONNECTION
                                Beatrice Ross Buszek

Basted with a piquant sauce, this baked dish is flavorful and succulent.

Sweet and Tangy Chicken

⅓ cup melted butter or margarine
3 tablespoons Worcestershire sauce
1 small clove garlic, peeled and minced
½ cup any tart red jelly
2 teaspoons prepared mustard
1 teaspoon sugar
3 drops Tabasco sauce
¼ teaspoon salt
1 frying chicken (3 pounds), cut up

Combine all ingredients except chicken. Place over low heat and cook until jelly has melted and sauce has blended smoothly. Arrange chicken in a baking pan, skin side up. Pour sauce over evenly. Cover pan with foil and bake 30 minutes in a 400° F oven; uncover pan and bake 30 minutes longer, or until chicken is tender and well browned. Baste with pan juices twice during last half hour of baking. Serve hot with the pan sauce spooned over each serving.

Serves 4   THE LADIES AID COOKBOOK
Beatrice Vaughan

Chicken breasts rolled around ham and Swiss cheese, covered with a cranberry-sauterne mixture and topped with toasted sliced almonds. An easy special-occasion entrée.

Fort Anne Chicken

3 large chicken breasts (boned, skinned, halved lengthwise)
6 thin slices boiled ham
4 ounces Swiss cheese (six 3 × ½ inch sticks)
1 can whole cranberry sauce
¼ cup all-purpose flour
3 tablespoons butter
⅓ cup sauterne
2 tablespoons cornstarch
2 tablespoons cold water
toasted sliced almonds

Pound chicken lightly to make cutlets, ¼ inch. Sprinkle with salt. Place ham slice, cheese stick and one tablespoon cranberry sauce on each one. Roll as for jelly roll.

Coat with flour. Brown in butter. Remove to 12 × 7 × 2 baking dish. In same skillet, combine cranberry and sauterne. Pour over chicken. Cover and bake 1 hour at 350° F. Remove to hot platter.

Combine cornstarch and cold water. Add pan juices and cook quickly, until thick. Spoon some of the sauce over chicken. Top with almonds. Pass remaining sauce.

Serves 6   THE CRANBERRY CONNECTION
                              Beatrice Ross Buszek

Juicy oven-barbecued chicken.

Paper-Bag Barbecued Chicken

¼ cup melted vegetable shortening
1 (3-pound) frying chicken, cut up
1 cup barbecue sauce*

Open a large, heavy paper bag (be sure there are no holes in it) and place it on its side on a large baking pan. With pastry brush, brush melted shortening over the inside of the bag, covering well. Place chicken pieces skin side up in a single layer on the bottom of the bag. Spoon barbecue sauce evenly over the chicken; fold the open end of the bag over twice and secure the closure with paper clips. Place the pan in a cold oven, then set the temperature control at 350° F, and bake the chicken for 1¾ hours. *Do not open* the bag during cooking time. Remove pan from oven and slit open the bag, remove chicken to a serving platter. Spoon sauce in the bag over the chicken and serve at once.

Serves 4   THE LADIES AID COOKBOOK
                                                    Beatrice Vaughan
*See page 63.

Ten money-saving servings from one fowl.

Wonderful "Stretched" Chicken

1 fowl (about 5 pounds), cut up (or 2 small cut-up chickens)
1 small onion, peeled
salt*
7 cups whole-wheat breadcrumbs
3 tablespoons soft butter or margarine
salt and pepper to taste
1 cup finely diced celery
5 eggs
4 tablespoons flour
1 chicken bouillon cube

Cover chicken with lightly salted water, add the onion and simmer until tender; save the broth.

Remove the bones and skin and cut the chicken in small pieces (about 1-inch cubes). Season the crumbs with salt and pepper and blend in the butter; reserve 1 cup for the topping.

Boil the celery for 10 minutes in 1½ cups of the broth, then add it, with its cooking liquid plus enough more broth to make 3 cups, to 6 cups of the seasoned crumbs; stir to mix, and add 2 of the eggs, slightly beaten. Set the mixture aside.

Dissolve the bouillon cube in 3 cups of the broth and carefully blend in the flour; stir and cook gently until the broth is slightly thickened. Remove from the heat and quickly whisk in the remaining 3 eggs, well beaten; return to the heat and simmer and stir until thick; season to taste with salt and pepper; cool.

In a large, oblong baking pan (about 10 × 13 inches) make alternate layers of crumb dressing, cut-up chicken, and the cus-

*If you're using cut-up fryers, add 2 bouillon cubes to the water to make a more flavorful broth, and reduce the amount of salt in the water.

tard-like sauce; top with the reserved 1 cup of breadcrumbs. Bake in a 375° F oven until slightly bubbly — about 30 minutes.

Serves 10   PUTTING FOOD BY
Ruth Hertzberg, Beatrice Vaughan, Janet Greene

Keep a supply in the refrigerator. It stores well.

A Good Chicken Barbeque Sauce

1 cup catsup
½ cup water
¼ cup lemon juice
1 small onion, peeled and chopped
1 small clove of garlic, minced
1 teaspoon salt
¼ teaspoon pepper
1 teaspoon paprika
1 tablespoon light brown sugar
2 tablespoons vegetable oil

Combine all ingredients except the oil. Simmer for 15 minutes. Remove from heat and add oil. Enough for 2 good-sized broilers.

Makes about 2½ cups   THE LADIES AID COOKBOOK
Beatrice Vaughan

A delicious old-fashioned way of serving a fowl.

Chicken and Sour-Milk Dumplings

1 5–6 pound fowl
1 large onion, peeled and quartered
2 teaspoons salt
pinch of pepper
8 medium potatoes, peeled
8 medium onions, peeled and parboiled
flour for thickening gravy

Cut up fowl and place in a deep kettle which has a close-fitting lid. Add salt and pepper, the large onion and just enough water barely to cover the chicken. Cover and simmer fowl slowly for about 2 hours. Add potatoes and the 8 onions, which have been parboiled for 20 minutes in salted water and drained. Cover and continue cooking for about 30 minutes more. (The chicken should be tender by now, but if the fowl is an old one it may be necessary to add another 30 minutes of cooking time.) When fowl is fork-tender, mix dumplings and drop in by small spoonfulls on top of simmering chicken and vegetables. Cover tightly while cooking.

Remove chicken, dumplings and vegetables to a deep, hot platter. Skim fat from broth and thicken, using 5 tablespoons flour mixed to a paste with 5 tablespoons cold water, to 5 cups of broth. Simmer 3 minutes, stirring constantly. Arrange chicken in center of platter, surrounded by the vegetables and dumplings. Pour gravy over all and serve at once.

Sour-Milk Dumplings

2 cups thick sour milk
½ teaspoon baking soda
2 eggs, beaten
1 scant teaspoon salt
pinch of pepper
about 3–3½ cups flour

Add soda to the sour milk, then add beaten eggs. Sift salt and pepper with 2½ cups flour and stir into the milk mixture. Add enough more sifted flour ¼ cup at a time to make dough stiff enough to drop from spoon. (The amount of flour will vary according to the consistency of milk: very thick sour milk requires less flour than does the thin sour milk. In general, dumpling batter should be a little stiffer than muffin batter, but not quite so stiff as biscuit dough.)

Drop dumplings carefully so that they rest on the chicken and vegetables and do not touch each other. Do not lift cover while dumplings are cooking. Cook dumplings 20 minutes if large, about 12 minutes if dumplings are quite small.

Serves 6–8   Yankee Hill-Country Cooking
Beatrice Vaughan

Sausage spices up leftover turkey.

Turkey-Sausage Puff

1 pound bulk sausage
½ cup minced onion
1 cup diced celery
2 eggs, beaten
1 cup milk
2 cups soft breadcrumbs
1 teaspoon poultry seasoning
3 cups leftover turkey gravy
2 cups diced, cooked turkey
salt and pepper to taste

Cook the sausage over moderate heat until nearly done but not browned, breaking the meat apart with a fork. Pour off the fat, leaving about 2 tablespoons in the pan; add onion and celery and continue cooking for about 5 minutes.

Combine beaten eggs, milk, breadcrumbs, poultry seasoning and 1 cup of the gravy. Stir in the turkey. Taste and add salt and pepper as needed. Stir in the sausage mixture, turn into a greased 10 × 7 baking pan, and bake in a 350° F oven for about 45 minutes, or until set and browned. Remove from oven and let stand 10 minutes. Serve with remaining gravy, heated.

Serves 6–8   THE LADIES AID COOKBOOK
                                                   Beatrice Vaughan

Cold and refreshing as a sea breeze on a hot day.

Jellied Chicken Loaf

1 frying chicken (2–3 pounds), cut up
1 large stalk celery
1 medium onion, peeled and quartered
2 teaspoons salt
1 teaspoon ground ginger
8 peppercorns
2 cups hot water
1 envelope plain gelatin
¼ cup cold water
¼ cup mayonnaise or salad dressing
2 teaspoons soy sauce
½ cup finely chopped celery
1 large canned pimiento, minced

Place cut-up chicken in large kettle and add next six ingredients. Cover and simmer gently until chicken is very tender, about 1 hour. Remove chicken from broth and cool.

Strain broth and add water, if needed, to make 2 cups of liquid. Soften the gelatin in the cold water, then add to the hot broth. Stir to dissolve, then remove from heat. Add mayonnaise and soy sauce. Cool, then chill until syrupy.

When chicken is cool, remove skin, bones and fat. Chop meat fine and add to gelatin mixture. Add celery and pimiento. Pour into a 1½ quart loaf pan and refrigerate for several hours. Unmold on lettuce and garnish with sliced tomatoes.

Serves 6   THE LADIES AID COOKBOOK
Beatrice Vaughan

A flavorful sauce for leftover chicken.

Gingered Sweet-Sour Sauce

1 tablespoon peanut or salad oil
2 green onions, chopped
1 clove garlic, crushed
rind from 1 orange, cut into thin strips
1 teaspoon minced or grated gingerroot
¾ cup chicken broth or bouillon
1½–2 tablespoons cornstarch
¼ cup each sake and fruit juice (pineapple, orange,
    grapefruit)
3 tablespoons cider vinegar
About 1 tablespoon soy sauce
1–2 tablespoons honey to taste

Heat oil in wok or skillet. Sauté green onions and garlic until softened but not brown. Add orange rind and gingerroot. Stir in broth; bring to a boil; cover and simmer 5 to 10 minutes. Blend cornstarch with sake; gradually stir into hot mixture. Bring to full boil, stirring, until mixture thickens. Cook, stirring, 1 minute. Remove from heat. Stir in remaining ingredients. Adjust honey to taste.

   Or use this sauce for chicken with broccoli, carrots, and mushrooms that are first stir-fried in a wok, then simmered in the broth before the cornstarch is added. The sauce is also delicious over shrimp and fish. It has the ability to transform odds and ends of ingredients into a proud Chinese main dish when served over cooked rice.

Makes about 1½ cups sauce   THE COOK'S ADVISOR
                                             Camille J. Stagg

Fish, onion, zucchini, tomatoes, and spaghetti in a casserole.

Fillets Italiano

2 pounds fish fillets
½ cup sliced onions
1 tablespoon garlic powder
¼ cup olive oil
2 cups sliced zucchini
2 tablespoons flour
½ teaspoon salt
¼ teaspoon pepper
1 1-pound can tomatoes
1 8-ounce can tomato sauce
1 teaspoon basil
½ teaspoon oregano
2 cups cooked spaghetti
½ cup grated Parmesan cheese

Cut fish into 1-inch chunks. Cook onions in 2 tablespoons of the oil until tender. Add garlic powder and fish; cook until fish is lightly browned. Remove from pan. Add remaining olive oil and zucchini to pan and heat thoroughly. Add flour, salt, and pepper; mix well. Add tomatoes, tomato sauce, basil, and oregano. Cook until sauce is thickened and zucchini is almost tender. Layer spaghetti, fish mixture, and cheese in baking dish. Cover tightly with aluminum foil. Bake in 350° F oven for 20 minutes. Uncover and continue baking about 20 minutes until zucchini is tender and fish flakes easily.

Serves 4

Fish Cookery
James Vilkitis and Susan Uhlinger

An unusual fish loaf served with lemony cranberry sauce.

Baked Fish Loaf with Cranberry Sauce

2½ cups cooked fish flakes
1½ cups soft bread cubes
1 cup milk
3 eggs, beaten
1 cup chopped celery
½ cup chopped onions
2 tablespoons melted butter or olive oil
2 tablespoons chopped pimiento
1 teaspoon Worcestershire sauce
4 tablespoons lemon juice
1 teaspoon salt

Combine bread cubes, milk, and eggs; mix. Cook celery and onions in butter until tender. Add pimiento, Worcestershire sauce, lemon juice, salt, and fish to bread mixture. Combine with celery and onions and mix well. Press evenly into greased loaf pan, 9 × 5 inches. Bake in 350° F oven about 70 minutes or until mixture is set. Let stand 10 minutes before turning out of pan. Serve with Cranberry Sauce.

Serves 5–6

Cranberry Sauce

1 tablespoon sugar
1 tablespoon cornstarch
1 1-pound can whole cranberry sauce
¾ cup water
1 tablespoon lemon juice
1 teaspoon grated lemon rind

Combine sugar and cornstarch; add cranberry sauce, water, and lemon juice. Stirring constantly, cook until thick and clear. Stir in lemon rind.

Makes about 1¾ cups sauce   FISH COOKERY
James Vilkitis and Susan Uhlinger

Layered with shrimp, cheese, and olives, this is a seafood-cheese special.

Shrimp and Cheese Casserole

6 slices stale bread, crusts removed
1½ tablespoons softened butter or margarine
7-ounce package frozen, shelled shrimps, thawed
½ cup sliced stuffed olives
1 cup shredded store (Cheddar) cheese (¼ pound)
3 eggs, beaten
pinch each of salt and dry mustard
3 drops Tabasco sauce
2½ cups milk
paprika

Spread bread lightly with the butter, then cut in cubes. Place half the cubes in a buttered casserole. Cut the shrimps coarsely and scatter over the bread. In layers add olives, cheese and remaining bread cubes.

Beat eggs, salt, mustard, Tabasco and milk together; pour over all. Sprinkle top lightly with paprika, bake in 325° F oven for about 25 minutes or until puffed and brown.

Serves 4–6   STORE-CHEESE COOKING
Beatrice Vaughan

Horseradish, sour cream, and dill dress this summery salad.

Marinated Fish Salad

2 cups cooked fish flakes
1 small onion, sliced
⅓ cup lemon juice
¼ cup olive oil
½ teaspoon garlic powder
½ teaspoon chopped parsley
½ cup sliced green onion tops
2 cups diced cucumbers
2 tablespoons diced pimiento
2 cups chopped celery
1 cup sour cream
¼ cup horseradish
1 teaspoon dill
⅛ teaspoon pepper
crisp salad greens
cucumber sticks and tomato wedges for garnish

Place fish, onion, lemon juice, olive oil, garlic powder, parsley, onion tops, cucumbers, pimiento, and celery in bowl. Cover and chill 1 to 2 hours. Combine sour cream, horseradish, dill, and pepper; mix well. Drain fish and vegetables; gently fold in sour cream mixture. Serve on crisp salad greens with cucumber and tomato garnish.

Serves 4–6   FISH COOKERY
                                          James Vilkitis and Susan Uhlinger

A North African delight for a summer night.

Tunisian Mixed Salad

3 fairly small boiling potatoes, unpeeled
3 medium carrots, peeled and cut in thirds
1½ cups bite-size pieces of raw cabbage (the thick center
  leaves will remain crunchy)
10 medium radishes, thinly sliced
10 cherry tomatoes, halved (or 2 medium tomatoes, cut in
  wedges)
1 package (10 ounces) frozen artichoke hearts, cooked as
  directed
2 or 3 hard-boiled eggs, peeled and quartered
1 can (7 ounces) solid white tuna
8 black Greek olives
8 anchovy fillets
1 tablespoon lemon juice
⅛ teaspoon cinnamon
⅔ cup French dressing

Cut the potatoes in two, put them with the carrots in a large
saucepan, cover with lightly salted water and bring to a boil.
Cook over medium-low heat about 20 minutes. Add the cabbage
for the last 1 minute of cooking. Remove and drain the vegetables. The potatoes and carrots should be firm; the cabbage
should still crunch. Peel the potatoes and cut them, and the
carrots, into 1-inch cubes.
  In a large bowl combine the lemon juice, French dressing, and
cinnamon. Add the potatoes, carrots, cabbage, and artichoke
hearts, stir and refrigerate to chill. When ready to serve, add
the radishes, olives and tomatoes and mix well. Transfer the
salad to a platter, surrounding it with the quartered eggs, each
draped with an anchovy fillet, and the chunks of tuna.

Serves 5–6   SALADS
                                                         Suzanne Best

Theme and variations for a hot-weather salad.

Mediterranean Rice Salad

1½ cups cooked long-grain rice, still warm
3 medium tomatoes, cut in ½-inch squares (or 15 cherry
    tomatoes, quartered)
½ cup finely chopped parsley leaves
½ cup finely diced cucumber
2 tablespoons minced red onion (or 3 tablespoons scallions,
    finely chopped)
½ pound (minimum) cooked fresh shrimp, shelled
1 can (7 ounces) chunk tuna fish, drained
⅓ cup green olive condite, coarsely chopped (or 1 jar [6
    ounces] marinated artichokes, drained and cut in bite-
    size chunks, 1 tablespoon capers and 6 green olives,
    coarsely chopped)
⅔ cup French dressing
1 tablespoon lemon juice
1 head romaine or Boston lettuce (or 2 heads Bibb)

Place the warm rice in a bowl with half the French dressing, stir
and chill. If using medium or large shrimp, slice them in half
lengthwise. When the rice is chilled, add all the remaining ingredients, mix well, and mound on a bed of lettuce.

Serves 4   SALADS
                                                Suzanne Best

Two excellent variations for Mediterranean Rice Salad: 1) Instead of tuna and shrimp,
use 1½ cups ham and 1½ cups chicken, cut in bite-size pieces. 2) Make an all-
vegetable rice salad to accompany any simply prepared meat or fish. Include all
or most of the vegetables listed above and an assortment of the following: ½
cup finely chopped raw mushrooms, raw zucchini, or beets; also ½ cup baby
peas; ¼ cup finely chopped green pepper, water chestnuts, or pimiento, or
pickled lemons.

Inexpensive and easy to make. Good idea for a potluck supper.

Deviled Clams

¼ cup plus 2 tablespoons melted butter or margarine
¼ cup minced onions
¼ cup minced celery
1 clove garlic, peeled and minced
1 tablespoon flour
1 tablespoon catsup
½ teaspoon salt
pinch of pepper
¼ teaspoon thyme
3 drops Tabasco sauce
2 (7-ounce) cans minced clams, undrained
1 beaten egg
1 cup fine dry breadcrumbs
2 tablespoons chopped parsley
paprika

Simmer ¼ cup butter, the onion, celery and garlic for about 5 minutes. Stir in flour and catsup, then add the seasonings. Add clams and bring just to boiling point. Add ½ cup of the crumbs, the parsley and the beaten egg. Bring to boiling point again, then pour into a buttered 1½ quart baking dish. Combine the remaining 2 tablespoons melted butter with the remaining ½ cup crumbs, scatter over the top of the clam mixture, and dust with paprika. Bake about 15 minutes in a 425° F oven or until golden brown and bubbling hot. Serve at once.

Serves 4–6   THE LADIES AID COOKBOOK
                                       Beatrice Vaughan

This goes together in a trice.

Crabmeat Casserole

1 (7-ounce) can crabmeat
1 cup dry poultry stuffing mix
1 cup milk
1 cup creamy salad dressing
1 tablespoon minced parsley
1 tablespoon minced onion
6 hard-cooked eggs
1 cup cooked green peas
1 tablespoon melted butter or margarine
3 tablespoons dry breadcrumbs

Pick crabmeat into flakes, discarding tendons, and add stuffing mix, milk, salad dressing, parsley, and onion, mixing lightly. Shell and slice the eggs and fold them into the crabmeat mixture; fold in the peas. Turn into a greased casserole. Combine melted butter and breadcrumbs, sprinkle over the top and bake in a 375° F oven for about 35 minutes, or until top is browned and all is bubbling hot.

Serves 4–5
THE LADIES AID COOKBOOK
Beatrice Vaughan

Doused with a mixture of maple syrup, mustard, lemon juice, and curry, these broiled scallops are delectable.

Broiled Curried Scallops

2 pounds scallops
¼ cup maple syrup
¼ cup prepared mustard
1 teaspoon lemon juice
2 teaspoons curry powder

Line bottom of broiler pan with foil and arrange scallops in it. Combine thoroughly the syrup, mustard, lemon juice and curry powder. Brush tops of scallops with about half the mixture, slide pan under broiler at lowest level and broil 10 minutes. Turn each scallop, brush with remainder of syrup mixture. Return to broiler and broil 10 minutes.

Serves 5–6   REAL, OLD-TIME YANKEE MAPLE COOKING
Beatrice Vaughan

Vegetarian
Dishes

Cumin, coriander, and lemon juice give the filling its Middle Eastern flavor.

Middle Eastern Taco

10 pieces Middle Eastern pocket bread (pita) or 10 wheat
    tortillas
1 cup dry garbanzo beans, well cooked
½ cup (heaping) toasted ground sesame seeds or ¼ cup
    sesame butter
2 cloves garlic
2 tablespoons lemon juice
¾ teaspoon coriander, ground
salt
½ teaspoon cumin, ground
¼–½ teaspoon cayenne
Garnishes: shredded lettuce, chopped tomatoes, chopped onion,
1½ cups yogurt or cheese, chopped cucumber

Purée the garbanzo beans together with sesame seeds or sesame butter, garlic, lemon juice and spices. Increase spices to taste. Let mixture stand at least ½ hour at room temperature.

Cut pieces of pita bread in half, pull open "pockets" and fill with bean mixture. You may want to heat the filled bread in the oven before garnishing. Or serve on wheat tortillas, fried until soft but not crisp.

Add the garnishes or allow everyone at the table to assemble their own tacos.

Makes 10   Your Health Under Siege
                                Jeffrey Bland

A Mexican favorite.

Tostadas

5 cups cooked or canned pinto beans (2 cups dry beans)
oil for frying
1 dozen corn tortillas
½ pound Monterey Jack or Cheddar cheese, grated
½ head lettuce, shredded
1–2 fresh tomatoes, chopped
1 onion, finely chopped
green chili sauce or taco sauce
1 cup yogurt (optional)

In a deep, heavy skillet, heat 2–3 tablespoons of oil very hot. Then quickly add the beans with a wooden spoon (some liquid is added this way). The oil should be hot enough to toast the beans. Continue cooking at a high heat, all the time mashing with the back of the spoon. Add salt to taste. (*Refritos* is an idiom for "well-fried," not "refried.")

Fry each tortilla briefly in a little bit of oil or heat them until crisp in the oven. To assemble, spread a tortilla with a sizable amount of beans, then top with garnishes of cheese, lettuce, tomatoes, and onions. Top with sauce and a dab of yogurt.

Serves 6

YOUR HEALTH UNDER SIEGE
Jeffrey Bland

Tortillas, tomatoes, cheese, and beans are layered into this tasty casserole.

Enchilada Bake

1 onion, chopped
1 clove garlic, minced
5–6 mushrooms, sliced
1 green pepper, chopped
½ cup dry beans, cooked (about 1½ cups)
1½ cups stewed tomatoes
1 tablespoon chili powder
1 teaspoon cumin, ground
½ cup red wine
salt to taste
6–8 corn tortillas

Other Layers

½–1 cup Monterey Jack (or other) cheese
½–1 cup mixture of ricotta cheese and yogurt (or blended
    cottage cheese and yogurt)
Garnish: Black olives

Sauté in oil: onion, garlic, mushrooms, green pepper and cooked beans, until onion is translucent and pepper is just tender. Add tomatoes, chili powder, cumin, red wine and salt to taste. Simmer 30 minutes.

In an oiled casserole dish put a layer of tortillas, a layer of sauce, 3 tablespoons of grated cheese, 3 tablespoons of the cheese-yogurt mix. Repeat until all the ingredients are used, ending with the layer of sauce. Garnish the top with the cheese-yogurt mix and the black olives. Bake at 350° F for 15 to 20 minutes.

Serves 4   YOUR HEALTH UNDER SIEGE
                                              Jeffrey Bland

Sesame seeds and curry or chopped walnuts add to this vegetarian dish.

Legume Casserole

2 cups onion, chopped fine
8 tablespoons toasted, ground sesame seed with 1 table-
    spoon curry powder or ½ cup walnuts
1 cup dry garbanzos cooked with extra water (save 2 cups
    stock) or 3 cups cooked or canned beans
¼ cup oil
½ cup whole wheat flour
⅔ cup instant dry milk (½ cup if non-instant)
2 cups stock from beans, or water, seasoned
2 teaspoons salt

Sauté chopped onion in oil until transparent. Add sesame seed
with curry powder or walnuts, and continue to sauté for one
minute more. Mix well with beans and place in small, well-oiled
casserole.

To make sauce, heat oil in saucepan, add whole wheat flour
and stir until toasted and nutty smelling. Blend dry milk, stock
from beans and salt into flour mixture with a whisk. Simmer
sauce until thickened. Pour sauce over beans in casserole and
bake for 30 minutes in a 350° F oven.

Sprinkle chopped parsley on top.

Serves 4   Your Health Under Siege
                                            Jeffrey Bland

A savory sauce and vegetables turn the inexpensive soybean into an interesting one-dish meal.

Crusty Soybean Casserole

1 cup cooked soybeans
2 cups corn, fresh or frozen
2 cups canned tomatoes
1 cup chopped onion
½ cup chopped celery
1 clove garlic, crushed
½ teaspoon each thyme and summer savory
pinch cayenne
2 teaspoons salt
¼ cup tomato paste
3 tablespoons brewer's yeast
½ cup stock or water
2½ cups raw brown rice, cooked (about 5¾ cups)

Topping:
⅓ cup or more grated cheese
wheat germ
butter

Combine cooked soybeans with corn, tomatoes, onion, celery, garlic, herbs, cayenne and salt. Mix well.

Combine separately tomato paste, brewer's yeast and stock. Place half of the cooked rice on the bottom of an oiled 4–6 quart casserole. Cover with the vegetable mixture. Spread the tomato-paste mixture over the vegetables, and cover all with the rest of the rice. Sprinkle with grated cheese and then wheat germ. Dot with butter and bake uncovered for 30 minutes at 350° F.

Serves 6–8   YOUR HEALTH UNDER SIEGE
Jeffrey Bland

A colorful and healthful combination.

Roman Rice and Beans

2 cloves garlic, crushed
1 large onion, chopped
1-2 carrots, chopped
1 stalk celery or 1 green pepper, chopped
⅔ cup parsley, chopped
2-3 teaspoons dried basil
1 teaspoon oregano
2-3 coarsely chopped large tomatoes
2 teaspoons salt
pepper to taste
¾ cup dried beans (pea, kidney), cooked (about 2 cups)
2 cups raw brown rice, cooked with 2 teaspoons salt (about
    5 cups)
½ cup or more Parmesan cheese

Sauté garlic, onion, carrots, celery or green pepper in oil or butter. Add parsley, basil and oregano. Add tomatoes, salt and pepper to taste. Mix well with beans and heat mixture.

Mix Parmesan cheese into brown rice. Add bean mixture to rice mixture, tossing lightly. Garnish with more parsley and more grated cheese. Can be eaten hot or cold.

Serves 6　　　　　　　　　Your Health Under Siege
Jeffrey Bland

Bubbly and delicious.

Eggplant Party Casserole

2 medium-size eggplants
about 2 tablespoons salt (to draw out eggplant juice)
about ¼ cup vegetable oil (olive is best here)
2 medium onions, thinly sliced
2 cloves garlic, chopped fine
2 small unpeeled zucchini squash (about 7 inches), cut in ½-inch slices
1 quart (4 cups) canned whole tomatoes, drained, de-seeded and chopped
2 good-sized ribs of celery, chopped small
1 tablespoon fresh basil (or ½ teaspoon dried)
¼ cup chopped fresh parsley
scant ½ cup grated Parmesan cheese (1½ to 2 ounces)
1½ cups ½-inch fresh bread cubes (about 4 slices)
about 2 tablespoons more oil (for pan-toasting bread cubes)
1 cup (¼ pound) coarsely grated Mozzarella cheese

Slice eggplants in ½-inch slices; spread slices in a large cookie pan and sprinkle them rather generously with salt. Let stand for 10 minutes to draw out excess moisture, then rinse away the salt and pat each slice very dry. Cut slices in ½-inch cubes and brown them lightly in hot oil in the bottom of a heavy pot over moderate heat. Add onions, garlic and zucchini, and cook them together for 2 to 3 minutes, stirring and adding a bit more oil as needed. Add celery, tomatoes and basil, cover and simmer until the squash is tender — about 7 to 10 minutes — stirring occasionally. Remove the pot from heat, stir in the Parmesan cheese and parsley; add salt and pepper to taste.

Pour the vegetable mixture into a 3- to 4-quart casserole. Top with bread cubes, which have been lightly browned in about 2

tablespoons of hot oil in a heavy skillet, and sprinkle with the grated Mozzarella cheese over all. Bake uncovered in a preheated 375° F oven until it's bubbly and browned — about 30 minutes.

Serves 12–15   PUTTING FOOD BY
Ruth Hertzberg, Beatrice Vaughan, Janet Greene

Nice served with sliced ripe tomatoes.

Cheese Corn Rabbit

    1 cup canned cream-style corn
    2 tablespoons melted butter or margarine
    ½ cup shredded store (Cheddar) cheese
    ¼ teaspoon salt
    ¼ teaspoon ground mustard
    ¼ teaspoon paprika
    ½ cup milk
    1 egg, beaten

Combine corn, butter and cheese and cook over low heat until cheese has melted, stirring constantly. Add salt, mustard and paprika. Add milk to beaten egg and stir hot mixture into this. Return to heat and cook slowly until thick and creamy, stirring constantly. Serve at once, spooned over hot toast triangles.

Serves 4   THE OLD COOK'S ALMANAC
Beatrice Vaughan

Soybeans provide protein for a nicely seasoned casserole.

Meatless Moussaka

Base Layer

oil as needed
1 large eggplant, peeled and sliced
2 tablespoons butter
1 large onion, finely chopped
⅓ cup dry soybeans, cooked, seasoned, and puréed (1 cup)
½ cup raw brown rice, cooked (1½ cups)
3 tablespoons tomato paste
½ cup red wine
¼ cup chopped parsley
⅛ teaspoon cinnamon
salt and pepper
½ cup breadcrumbs
½ cup Parmesan cheese, grated

Sauté eggplant slices in oil. Set aside.

Sauté chopped onion in butter until translucent. Add beans, rice, tomato paste, red wine, parsley, cinnamon and salt and pepper to taste. Mix well.

In casserole make alternating layers of eggplant slices and rice and bean mixture. Sprinkle with breadcrumbs and Parmesan cheese.

Top Custard

4 tablespoons butter
3 tablespoons whole-wheat flour
2 cups milk
2 eggs
1 cup ricotta cheese or cottage cheese, blended smooth
nutmeg

Make a cream sauce by melting 4 tablespoons of butter and blending in the flour, stirring with a wire whisk. Then stir in the milk gradually, and continue stirring over low heat until the mixture thickens and is smooth. Remove from heat, cool slightly, and stir in the eggs, ricotta, and nutmeg.

Pour the sauce over all and bake about 45 minutes at 375° F, or until the top is golden and a knife comes out clean from the custard. Remove from the oven and cool 20 to 30 minutes before serving. Cut into squares and serve.

Serves 6   Your Health Under Siege
Jeffrey Bland

A meatless stroganoff made with yogurt instead of sour cream.

Lentil Stroganoff

½ cup onion, chopped
1 small clove garlic, chopped fine
½ pound fresh mushrooms, sliced
¼ cup safflower oil, soy, margarine, or butter
1 cup dry lentils
1 tablespoon tomato paste
2 tablespoons ground oat flour
¾ cup vegetable broth
2 teaspoons tamari (soy sauce)
1 cup low-fat, unflavored yogurt

Combine lentils with 2½ cups water. Bring to a boil; turn heat down to a simmer. Simmer about 45 minutes, until the lentils are tender but still maintain their shape.

Sauté the onion, garlic, and mushrooms in oil about 5 minutes. Add the cooked lentils, flour, broth, tomato paste, and soy sauce. Simmer several minutes and slowly add the yogurt, stirring constantly. Simmer 2 minutes, but do not boil. Serve over cooked whole-wheat noodles or cooked brown rice.

Serves 4–6   YOUR HEALTH UNDER SIEGE
                                            Jeffrey Bland

Note: Whole wheat noodles will not expand as much as white noodles. To cook them, simply put them in a pot of boiling water and boil until tender, about 7 to 10 minutes.

Mint, dill, and parsley perk up this skillet dinner served over brown rice.

Greek-Style Skillet

2 tablespoons olive oil
1 medium onion, chopped
1 clove garlic, minced
1 small or medium eggplant, peeled and diced (1-inch cubes)
½ to 1 teaspoon mint
½ to 1 teaspoon dillweed
1 tablespoon parsley flakes
juice of one lemon (2 tablespoons)
1 cup canned tomatoes
1 8-ounce can tomato sauce
¼ pound green beans or other green vegetables (not necessary but adds a beautiful touch)
1 cup raw brown rice, cooked with ¼ cup soy grits (3 cups)
yogurt

Sauté onion and garlic in oil until translucent. Add eggplant and sauté 5 minutes more. Add mint, dillweed and parsley. Add lemon juice, tomatoes and tomato sauce. Stir carefully but well. Add green beans.

Cover and cook on low heat 15 minutes. Serve the cooked mixture over rice, topping each serving with a spoonful of yogurt.

Serves 4
Your Health Under Siege
Jeffrey Bland

Cheese, hard-boiled eggs and mushrooms combine nicely.

Baked Cheese and Mushrooms

½ pound fresh mushrooms, cut up
1 small green pepper, seeded and cut up
3 tablespoons melted butter or margarine
⅔ cup soft breadcrumbs
¼ teaspoon salt
pinch of pepper
1 canned pimiento, cut up
1½ cups milk
1 cup shredded store (Cheddar) cheese (¼ pound)
5 hard-boiled eggs, cut up
2 tablespoons dry breadcrumbs for topping
1 tablespoon melted butter or margarine for topping
paprika

Simmer mushrooms and green pepper in the melted butter until tender, about 10 minutes. Stir in the soft breadcrumbs, salt, pepper, pimiento and milk; add cheese and eggs. Turn into buttered 1-quart casserole.

Combine the dry breadcrumbs with the melted butter, sprinkle over the top; shake paprika lightly over all. Bake in a 375° F oven for about 45 minutes or until golden and bubbling hot.

Serves 4–6   Store-Cheese Cooking
                                                    Beatrice Vaughan

A cheese and wheat germ topping make this eggplant dish special.

Sprout Stuffed Eggplant

2 cups sprouts, any kind (wheat, mung, or pea bean, rice, etc.)
1 large eggplant
2 tablespoons peanut, safflower or corn oil
1 small onion, diced
1 stalk celery, diced
1 tablespoon minced parsley
salt and pepper to taste
2 tablespoons grated cheese
2 tablespoons wheat germ

Cut eggplant in half lengthwise. Scoop out center, leaving about ½-inch shell. Put oil in small frying pan. Add onion and sauté until lightly brown. Dice center part of eggplant. Add sautéed onion, celery, parsley, salt and pepper. Mix well and stuff into eggplant shells. Put on greased baking sheet. Top with mixed cheese and wheat germ. Bake at 350° F for 45 to 50 minutes. Eggplant should be thoroughly cooked but not mushy. Serve with tomato sauce, if desired.

Serves 2

SPROUTS TO GROW AND EAT
Esther Munroe

A good way to use leftovers.

Vegetable Timbale

1 cup chicken stock or bouillon
½ cup half-and-half or milk
4 eggs, lightly beaten
¼ teaspoon salt
1½ tablespoons chopped parsley
1 green onion, minced
½ teaspoon dried leaf thyme
⅛ teaspoon lemon juice
*1 cup well-drained cooked spinach, chopped fine, puréed
   or sieved
2 tablespoons grated sharp cheese (Parmesan, Romano, etc.)
Cheese or hollandaise sauce

Blend ingredients through lemon juice with wire whisk. Stir in spinach and cheese. Pour into 6 or 7 buttered timbale molds or 4-oz. custard cups, or a 6-cup ring mold, filling about ¾ full. Arrange on rack in pan of hot water, adding enough water so level is even with top of timbale mixture in molds. Bake in a 325° F oven 25 to 30 minutes for individual molds, about 40 minutes for ring mold, or until knife inserted in center comes out clean. Loosen edges with sharp, thin-bladed knife and invert onto serving plates. If desired, top with a few watercress leaves; serve with a favorite sauce.

Serves 6

THE COOK'S ADVISOR
Camille J. Stagg

---

*Flaked or minced cooked, skinned, and boned lean fish or chicken, or a combination of vegetable and fish or chicken, can be substituted. Fish or chicken timbales are especially good with watercress, sorrel, or spinach sauce.

A warmer for a cold night.

Rinktum Tiddy

1 tablespoon butter
1 tablespoon chopped onion
1 quart canned stewed tomatoes, drained of their juice
2 well-beaten eggs to bind everything together
1 pound grated Cheddar cheese (4 cups)
salt, cayenne pepper and Worcestershire sauce to taste

In a 4-quart kettle simmer the onion in the butter until it is soft, add the drained tomatoes and continue to cook slowly for 10 minutes.

Meanwhile beat the egg, stir a bit of the hot tomato mixture into it, then return it to the tomato mixture along with the grated cheese. Stir over medium heat until the cheese is melted. Add the salt, cayenne pepper and Worcestershire sauce in amounts to please your taste. To serve, ladle over toast squares, crackers or cooked noodles.

Serves 6 easily   PUTTING FOOD BY
Ruth Hertzberg, Beatrice Vaughan, Janet Greene

A delicious curry, served over a brown rice-bulghur mixture.

Vegetable Curry

oil as needed
4 carrots, sliced diagonally
2 onions, sliced thinly
1 tablespoon (or more) hot curry powder
¼ cup flour
1 cup liquid from beans (or water)
¾ cup raisins
¾ cup cashews (raw or roasted)
3 tablespoons (or more) mango chutney
1 tablespoon brown sugar
⅔ cup dry soybeans, or kidneys, limas, or mix of the three,
    cooked (2 cups; save 1 cup bean liquid), or 2 cups
    canned beans
1 cup raw brown rice, cooked with ¾ cup raw bulghur (about
    3½ cups)

Sauté carrots and onions in small amount of oil until golden.
Add curry powder and flour; sauté for one minute. Add 1 cup
liquid from beans and simmer until carrots are tender but not
soft.

Add raisins, cashews, chutney, brown sugar, beans, and any
liquid needed to make a thick sauce. Adjust seasoning. Simmer
until the raisins are soft and the seasonings mingle.

Serve curry mixture over the cooked grain.

Serves 6   Your Health Under Siege
                                                        Jeffrey Bland

A nice way with zucchini. Fresh herbs make the difference.

Adele's Zucchini Pancakes

3 small or 1½ large zucchini, grated
A few finely chopped basil leaves and marjoram and savory
    sprigs
½ cup grated Cheddar cheese
1 cup whole-wheat flour, unsifted
1 teaspoon salt
1 teaspoon baking powder
1 lightly beaten egg
Dash of cayenne pepper
Enough milk and/or yogurt to make a thick batter

½ cup yogurt
½ cup sour cream

Combine all ingredients and fry pancakes in a lightly greased
iron skillet until golden brown on both sides. Serve with one-
half cup yogurt and one-half cup sour cream, well blended.

HEALTH, HAPPINESS AND THE PURSUIT OF HERBS
Adele Dawson

The lemony sauce makes this one.

Stuffed Zucchini

   10 medium zucchini
   ½ cup raw brown rice
   1 cup boiling water
   1½ cups chopped onion
   2 cups chopped celery
   1 cup chopped parsley
   2–3 teaspoons salt
   ½ cup olive oil
   1 cup breadcrumbs
   3 lemons
   2 eggs, separated
   pepper
Optional:
   1½ cups chopped mushrooms
   ½ cup grated Cheddar cheese

Hollow out the zucchini. Either make cylinders with an apple corer, or slice them in half lengthwise and scoop out the insides to make little boats. In either case, you will need a pan large enough to arrange them side by side for baking.

Chop all the vegetables very small. Chop the insides of the zucchini too, but keep them separate.

Cook the rice with water, onion, celery, salt, pepper, and oil for 15 minutes.

Add the chopped zucchini and cook 5 minutes more.

Add the breadcrumbs, parsley, juice from 2 of the lemons, and the whites of the eggs. Add mushrooms and cheese if desired.

Preheat oven to 350° F.

Put the filling into the scooped-out zucchini shells (If you chose the cylinder style, pack the filling in firmly with your fingers, keeping a bowl of cold water nearby to cool your hands.)

Arrange the zucchini in a baking dish. If there is extra filling, spread it over and around the zucchini. Cover and bake for about 40 minutes.

Beat the egg yolks with the remaining lemon juice. Spoon out some of the juices from the baking dish. Pour slowly into egg yolk-lemon mixture, stirring briskly. Return this sauce to the zucchini and bake for another 5 minutes.

Serves 6–8   YOUR HEALTH UNDER SIEGE
Jeffrey Bland

Vegetables

Tart apples, cherry or currant jelly, and vinegar add wonderful flavor to red cabbage. Superb with a holiday turkey or any roast poultry.

Braised Red Cabbage with Apples and Currant Jelly
Chou Rouge à la Flamande

5-pound head of red cabbage
3 quarts cold water
3 tablespoons coarse salt or 1½ tablespoons table salt
5 heaping tablespoons vegetable shortening
3–4 teaspoons table salt
7 tablespoons white vinegar
2½–3 pounds apples (Cortland or Baldwin)
1 12-ounce jar currant or cherry jelly

Remove base and outer leaves from cabbage; quarter; remove core. Wash under cold running water.

In the meantime, bring salted water to a rolling boil in a covered pot. If you do not have a kettle large enough to cook cabbage all at once, drop in half at a time. Wait until water again reaches a rolling boil and boil, uncovered, for 15 minutes. Transfer cooked cabbage to a colander (use slotted spoon or tongs if water is to be reused for other half of cabbage) and pass under cold running water. This stops the cooking action.

Squeeze moisture from a handful of cabbage, place on cutting board, and shred with a large knife. Repeat until all cabbage is shredded.

Dry the pot used for boiling with a paper towel; melt shortening in it over high heat. When it begins to smoke, sauté cabbage, tossing constantly with wooden spoon, for about 5 minutes.

Sprinkle cabbage with salt. Stir in the vinegar, 1 tablespoon at a time. The vinegar will restore the beautiful purple color to the cabbage as well as giving it a tart taste. Reduce heat, cover, and simmer for 60 minutes, tossing from time to time.

While the cabbage is cooking, peel, core, and quarter the apples. When the cabbage has cooked for 30 minutes add the apples and continue cooking.

Fifteen minutes after apples have been added, mix in the jelly. Cook the mixture 15 minutes longer. Taste, and if necessary, add another ¼ teaspoon of salt.

Serves 10–12   MY FRENCH KITCHEN
                               Denise Khaitman Schorr

Good with pork chops or meatloaf.

Cabbage with Sour-Cream Dressing

1 medium cabbage, shredded
pinch of baking soda
½ cup sour cream
1 tablespoon vinegar
1 tablespoon sugar
salt and pepper to taste

Cook cabbage for about 5 minutes in water to cover, to which the pinch of soda has been added. Drain and cover with freshly boiling water. Cook for 15 minutes more, then drain very well. Pour sour cream over hot cabbage, then add vinegar, sugar, salt and pepper. Mix all thoroughly. Serve at once.

Serves 6–8   YANKEE HILL-COUNTRY COOKING
                                    Beatrice Vaughan

Dried limas with built-in flavor.

Lima Beans Texas Style

1 pound dried lima beans
4 slices bacon
1 onion, chopped
1 rib celery, chopped
1 clove garlic, crushed
2 fresh tomatoes, chopped
3 teaspoons chili powder
1 tablespoon parsley, chopped
salt and pepper to taste

Soak the beans overnight; then boil gently in pot 2 hours or more until tender.

Fry the bacon until crisp and remove from the pan. Sauté the onion, celery and garlic in the bacon fat until light brown; add the tomatoes and cook 5 minutes. Add the chili powder, then the beans, drained (reserve the liquid). Continue cooking; add the parsley and crumbled bacon and season to taste. If the beans are too dry, add some of the liquid in which they were cooked.

Serves 6–8   FRESH VEGETABLES COOKBOOK
                    Eden Gray and Mary Beckwith Cohen

Wonderful with roast pork. Use more onions if you wish.

Baked Apples and Onions

12 medium tart apples, peeled and sliced
3 medium onions, peeled and sliced
2 tablespoons butter
1 teaspoon salt
pinch of pepper
½ cup dry breadcrumbs
1 tablespoon butter (for crumbs)
½ cup water

Place about half the apples in the bottom of a buttered deep baking dish which has a lid. Cover this layer of apples with half the onion slices, which have been separated into rings. Dot with 1 tablespoon of the butter and half the salt and pepper. Add a layer of the remaining apples, then the remaining onion slices and dot with remaining tablespoon butter and salt and pepper.

Toss crumbs in 1 tablespoon of butter, which has been melted. Sprinkle over top of onions and apples in baking dish. Add ½ cup water. Cover and bake slowly in 350° F oven until tender, about two hours. A little more water may be added if mixture begins to stick on during the baking.

Serves 8   YANKEE HILL-COUNTRY COOKING
Beatrice Vaughan

Delectable.

Whipped Potatoes with Swiss Cheese
Purée de Pommes de Terre

10–11 cups cubed potatoes, preferably Maine or Long Island
  (about 5½ pounds)
6 cups cold water
3 tablespoons coarse salt or 1½ tablespoons table salt
¾ pound whipped sweet butter (at room temperature)
2 cups warm milk
3 cups (about ¾ pound) grated imported Swiss cheese

Peel potatoes and cut into 1-inch cubes. Drop into large pot with cold water. This may be done a day ahead and the potatoes stored in the refrigerator.

To cook, add salt, cover pot, and bring to boiling point over moderate heat. Boil 20 minutes. Test for softness by inserting blade of small knife into a cube.

Pour contents into colander to drain off water. Return potatoes to pot; place over low heat. Using a potato masher, mash a small portion at a time and set to one side of pan so that they will be light and fluffy. When all have been mashed, remove pot from heat. Add butter, a tablespoon at a time, mixing in with wooden spoon. Next add milk and cheese alternately, a little at a time, stirring well after each addition with wooden spoon. *It is important to add these ingredients slowly, otherwise texture will be runny.*

When all ingredients have been carefully incorporated, keeping mixture over very low heat, whip with electric hand mixer at high speed for 1 minute.

Transfer potatoes to a heated covered vegetable dish; swirl fork over surface in a decorative pattern.

Serves 12

MY FRENCH KITCHEN
Denise Khaitman Schorr

Grated orange and lemon rind in a translucent citrus juice sauce adds tang to beets.

Orange-Lemon Beets

1½ tablespoons cornstarch
½ cup fresh lemon juice
½ cup fresh orange juice
2 tablespoons vinegar
2 tablespoons sugar
1 teaspoon salt
about 4 cups sliced cooked beets
1 teaspoon grated lemon rind
1 teaspoon grated orange rind
3 tablespoons butter or margarine

Blend cornstarch with the lemon juice, orange juice and vinegar. Stir over low heat until mixture boils and looks translucent. Remove from heat and add sugar and salt. Add beets. Simmer over low heat for about 15 minutes, stirring frequently. Stir in grated rinds and the butter. Serve hot.

Serves 4–6

CITRUS COOKING
Beatrice Vaughan

Small patty pan squash (2–3 inches in diameter) are the best to use in this Gallic treat.

Crown Squash au Gratin
Pâtisson Blanc Américain

Boiling the Squash

    2 pounds crown squash (patty pan squash)
    3 quarts cold water
    1½ tablespoons coarse salt or ¾ tablespoon table salt

Wash squash in cold water, changing water several times. Stems are short, so do not remove them; they add to the attractiveness of the finished dish.

Bring salted water to a rolling boil with cover on. Drop squash in; bring again to rolling boil and boil uncovered over high heat for about 7 minutes. (If squash are large, cooking time will be longer.) When small knife blade glides in and out easily, they are done.

Baking the Squash

    1 pat unsalted butter
    salt and pepper
    1½ to 2 teaspoons grated Swiss cheese per squash
    1–1½ teaspoons unsalted butter per squash
    6–8 teaspoons chopped parsley

Preheat oven to 450° F.

Coat a baking dish, large enough to hold squash uncrowded, with butter.

Cut squash in half horizontally; scoop out seeds with spoon. Place bottom halves in baking dish, cutting a bit off bottoms if necessary to make them rest evenly.

Sprinkle with salt, pepper, and cheese; dot with butter. Place stem halves on top; sprinkle with cheese; dot with butter. Bake 12 minutes.

Sprinkle with parsley.

Serves 4   MY FRENCH KITCHEN
                                                   Denise Khaitman Schorr

An old-fashioned favorite.

Deviled Carrots

    3 tablespoons brown sugar
    1 tablespoon prepared mustard
    pinch of salt
    2 tablespoons butter, melted
    3 cups hot, cooked carrots, sliced

Combine brown sugar, mustard, salt, and butter. Mix with carrots. Heat very hot, being careful not to scorch.

Serves 6   THE OLD COOK'S ALMANAC
                                                   Beatrice Vaughan

Young fern fronds served up au gratin. For tips on hunting fiddleheads, see p. 128.

Fiddleheads au Gratin

4 cups fiddleheads
1 cup water
½ cup grated Swiss cheese
1 celery stalk, minced
½ cup breadcrumbs
salt and pepper to taste

Boil the fiddleheads for 1 minute, then simmer for 10 minutes. Drain carefully. Place in a casserole dish. Sprinkle with the cheese. Cover the cheese with a second layer of fiddleheads and the celery. Top with the breadcrumbs.

Bake at 275° F for about 15 minutes. Serve hot as a side dish.

Serves 4–5   THE NATURAL WORLD COOKBOOK
Joe Freitus

A delicious way to serve a spring delicacy.

Fiddleheads Vinaigrette

3 cups fiddlehead tips
3 tablespoons vinegar
⅓ cup salad oil
1½ teaspoons chopped parsley
2 teaspoons finely chopped onion
1 teaspoon finely chopped pimiento
¼ teaspoon salt
pinch of pepper
½ teaspoon prepared mustard
½ teaspoon paprika

Wash the fiddleheads and boil in salted water until tender.
Drain. Mix together all of the above ingredients. Place the
cooked fiddleheads in a serving dish and cover with the sauce.
Serve while the fiddleheads are hot. An excellent side dish.

Serves 5   THE NATURAL WORLD COOKBOOK
                                           Joe Freitus

Bulghur, available in most markets, provides a nice change of pace. The mushrooms accent its nutty flavor.

Mushroom-Wheat Pilaf

½ cup butter or margarine (1 stick)
1 small onion, peeled and diced
½ pound fresh mushrooms, sliced
1 cup bulghur (cracked wheat)
1¼ cups chicken broth
salt to taste
1 cup chopped cooked chicken or turkey (optional)

Melt butter in a saucepan, then add onion and mushrooms. Simmer over low heat until tender and golden brown, stirring occasionally. Add bulghur and chicken broth, cover the pan and simmer over very low heat until bulghur is tender and broth absorbed. Stir often to prevent scorching. Add salt, if needed. If desired, add chicken. Heat very hot and serve.

Serves 4   THE LADIES AID COOKBOOK
                                         Beatrice Vaughan

Poultry stuffing and mashed potatoes combine for an interesting accompaniment to meats.

Stuffed Potato Casserole

1 small onion, peeled and minced
2 tablespoons melted butter or margarine
1 cup dry poultry stuffing
1 egg
½ cup milk
½ teaspoon salt
pinch of pepper
2 cups seasoned mashed potato

Simmer onion in the melted butter for 5 minutes, then stir in the dry stuffing. Beat the egg with the milk, salt and pepper, blend in the mashed potatoes, then combine with the stuffing mixture. Mix well, turn into a greased 1½ quart casserole, and bake uncovered until puffed and brown, about 30 minutes, in a 375° F oven.

Serves 6   THE LADIES AID COOKBOOK
                                                  Beatrice Vaughan

A good dish for a snowy night.

Tomato-Corn Pudding

  2 cups canned cream-style corn
  1 cup canned tomatoes, undrained
  1 beaten egg
  ¼ cup saltine cracker crumbs
  ½ teaspoon seasoned salt
pinch of pepper
  1 tablespoon minced onion
  1 tablespoon minced green pepper
  1 tablespoon melted butter or margarine

Combine all ingredients in order, then turn into a buttered 1½-quart baking dish. Bake uncovered in a 400° F oven for about 30 minutes. Remove from oven and let stand 10 minutes before serving.

Serves 6   PUTTING FOOD BY
Ruth Hertzberg, Beatrice Vaughan, Janet Greene

A refreshing change from candied sweet potatoes.

Cider-Baked Sweet Potatoes

4 medium sweet potatoes, peeled
1 large apple, peeled and sliced thin
¼ cup light brown sugar
1 teaspoon grated orange rind
3 tablespoons butter or margarine
⅔ cup sweet cider

Cook sweet potatoes in salted water until just barely tender. Drain and cut in thick slices. In greased, 1½-quart casserole place half of the potato slices, then add the apple slices. Combine grated rind with brown sugar, sprinkle half of it over the sweet potatoes and apples and dot with half of the butter. Cover with remaining sweet potato slices, top with remaining sugar and butter. Heat cider to boiling and pour over all. Bake in 375° F oven for about 1 hour, basting frequently with pan juices.

Serves 6   REAL, OLD-TIME YANKEE APPLE COOKING
Beatrice Vaughan

Delicious and elegant with roast chicken.

Wild Rice-Apricot Pilaf

2 cups cooked wild rice
¾ cups chopped dried apricots
3 tablespoons minced onion
3 tablespoons minced green pepper
salt to taste
1 chicken-flavored bouillon cube
3½ cups boiling water
1 tablespoon butter or margarine

Combine the apricots, onion, green pepper and salt in a saucepan. Dissolve the bouillon cube in the boiling water, stir into the apricot mixture and cook for 30 minutes or until the vegetables are soft. Add the rice and butter. Stir until the butter melts, then turn into a casserole dish.

Bake at 350° F until the liquid is absorbed.

Serves 5–6   THE NATURAL WORLD COOKBOOK
Joe Freitus

Good topped with sour cream or yogurt.

Potato Mushroom Pancakes

½ pound mushrooms
4 medium potatoes
1 medium onion
1 egg
1 teaspoon salt
⅛ teaspoon white pepper
1 teaspoon cornstarch
2 tablespoons flour
1 teaspoon baking powder

Peel the potatoes, slice or dice and purée in a blender; drain in a paper towel in a sieve.

Grate the onion in a large bowl; add the egg and other ingredients, except for the mushrooms, along with the drained potatoes. When the batter is stirred smooth, slice the mushrooms very fine and fold into the batter. Cook in a skillet in ¼ inch of hot oil, and drain briefly on a paper towel when cooked.

Makes 14–16 pancakes

PAN AND GRIDDLE CAKES
Samuel R. Ogden

Fill with creamed chicken, fish, or chipped beef.

Potato Patty Shells

    2 cups hot mashed potatoes (about 4 medium)
    1 egg, beaten
    1 tablespoon cream
    1 teaspoon baking powder
    2 tablespoons butter, melted
    ¾ teaspoon salt
    pinch of pepper

Add cream to beaten egg, then add melted butter, baking powder, salt, and pepper. Beat egg mixture into mashed potatoes and continue beating until light and fluffy. Use ⅓ cup of the mixture for each patty shell, forming small round mounds on a greased baking sheet. Make a depression on the top of each mound with the back of a tablespoon. Bake in 400° F oven until each patty shell is nicely browned, about 10 minutes.

Makes 6 shells. (If preferred, ½ cup may be used to make each shell, in which case the yield will be 4 large shells.)

YANKEE HILL-COUNTRY COOKING
Beatrice Vaughan

Layers of sweet potatoes and sliced oranges alternate. Especially good with ham.

Orange Sweet Potatoes

6 medium sweet potatoes, cooked and peeled
2 medium seedless oranges, unpeeled
¼ cup butter or margarine
½ cup light brown sugar
¼ cup honey
juice of 2 medium oranges
⅓ cup fine dry breadcrumbs

Cut potatoes in ¼-inch slices. Slice oranges thin, discarding the end slices. In buttered casserole, make alternating layers of the potatoes and the oranges. Sprinkle each layer with some of the butter and the sugar, reserving 2 tablespoons of the butter and 1 tablespoon of the sugar. Combine honey and orange juice. Stir over low heat until warm, then pour over potatoes and oranges. Melt the reserved 2 tablespoons butter and combine with the reserved 1 tablespoon sugar; mix with the dry crumbs and scatter evenly over surface. Cover and bake in a 350° F oven for about 20 minutes. Remove cover and bake about 40 minutes longer.

Serves 6

CITRUS COOKING
Beatrice Vaughan

Summer squash is cubed, sautéed slowly in butter with onion and sauced with sour cream.

Summer Squash with Sour Cream

2 medium summer squashes, unpeeled
1 teaspoon salt
1 medium onion, peeled and diced
¼ cup butter
2 cups sour cream
2 tablespoons flour
salt and pepper to taste

Cut squashes into 1-inch cubes and sprinkle with the 1 teaspoon salt. Let stand for about one hour, then drain away liquid drawn from squash by the salt.

Melt butter in a large frying pan and add diced onions and cubes of squash. Cook very slowly until squash is tender — about 30 minutes — stirring from time to time. Mix sour cream with flour and add to squash, simmering until all is hot, about 5 minutes. Season to taste with salt and pepper.

Serves 6   YANKEE HILL-COUNTRY COOKING
                                            Beatrice Vaughan

Applesauce, raisins, lemon, brown sugar, and cinnamon turn plain squash into something special.

Baked Winter Squash with Raisins

1 Hubbard (yellow) or 2 acorn squash
4 tablespoons brown sugar or honey
2 tablespoons butter or vegetable oil
2 cups applesauce
⅓ cup raisins
2 teaspoons lemon juice
1 teaspoon cinnamon

Cut the squash in half lengthwise, remove the seeds and membranes, and sprinkle with salt. Mix the rest of the ingredients in a bowl and spoon the mixture into the squash hollows. Bake at 375° F in a pan with sides, covering the squash with foil for the first 30 minutes; remove the foil and bake uncovered another 30 minutes, or until the squash is tender.

Serves 4–6
FRESH VEGETABLES COOKBOOK
Eden Gray and Mary Beckwith Cohen

Another tasty way with wild rice.

Wild Rice and Baked Onion Slices

3 cups cooked wild rice
4 large onions
3 beef-flavored bouillon cubes
2 cups boiling water
2 tablespoons melted butter or margarine
salt to taste

Peel the onions and slice thinly. Place in a shallow baking dish. Dissolve the bouillon cubes completely in the boiling water. Pour the broth over the onion slices. Bake at 375° F until tender, about 1 hour. Do not allow the broth to dry up.

Arrange the cooked rice in a serving dish. Cover with the baked onion rings. Stir the melted butter and salt into the remaining sauce and pour over the onion rings and rice.

Serves 5–6   THE NATURAL World COOKBOOK
Joe Freitus

Soufflés perk up a meal. Try this with different vegetables: asparagus, carrots, cauliflower, celery, eggplant, onions, or peas.

Basic Vegetable Soufflé

1 cup hot cream sauce
1 cup minced, drained cooked vegetables (or canned)
3 eggs separated
salt and pepper to taste

Combine hot cream sauce with the vegetables and heat to just below boiling point. Beat egg yolks until fluffy, then beat in the hot mixture. Season to taste with salt and pepper. Fold in stiffly beaten egg whites. Bake in a buttered 1½-quart casserole in a 325° F oven for about 45 minutes. Serve hot.

Serves 4   Putting Food By
Ruth Hertzberg, Beatrice Vaughan, Janet Greene

Salads

Vitamin-rich sprouts combine with vegetables, Swiss cheese, hard-boiled eggs, and bacon for a hearty salad.

Artichoke and Egg Salad

   1 cup mung bean sprouts
   6–8 cooked artichoke hearts, sliced
   ⅓ cup shredded raw carrot
   ⅓ cup shredded Swiss cheese
   3 strips bacon, fried crisp and crumbled
   2 hard-boiled eggs, sliced
   dressing of choice

Combine all ingredients, toss thoroughly and serve chilled. Salad may be served on beds of salad greens or just as is.

Serves 2–3   Sprouts to Grow and Eat
                                          Esther Munroe

Note: Hold back on adding the dressing and salad may be kept in the refrigerator for several hours before serving.

An old favorite dressed up with apples, grated orange rind, and spices.

Spicy Apple Cole Slaw

⅓ cup mayonnaise or salad dressing
½ cup dairy sour cream
1 teaspoon grated orange rind
1 tablespoon orange juice
pinch each of cinnamon, ground cloves and salt
1 tablespoon sugar
about 6 cups shredded cabbage
2 medium red eating apples, unpeeled

Combine mayonnaise, sour cream, orange juice, and grated rind. Add salt, spices, and sugar, mixing thoroughly. Pour over the cabbage, mixing in gently but thoroughly. Cover bowl and chill.

Just before serving, slice the apples in very thin slivers. Toss lightly with the cabbage. Serve at once.

Serves 6–8   REAL, OLD-TIME YANKEE APPLE COOKING
Beatrice Vaughan

The very first vegetable to tantalize us with the promise of summer is the luscious fiddlehead fern, which emerges not long after the snows disappear. Pick fiddleheads when they are still tightly curled and no more than 4–6 inches tall. Be sure to find Ostrich ferns, which are usually identifiable by their tall, dried-up brown plumes left from the previous year's growth. If you are unsure of yourself, get an experienced fern-hunter to show you which variety is edible. Rub the papery covering off gently, then parboil the ferns for a few minutes in water to cover. Drain, rinse, and you are ready to make a salad of marinated fiddleheads, or to fix them as a hot side dish.

Fiddlehead Salad

3 cups (or more) fiddleheads
1 onion sliced in rings
1 cucumber, thinly sliced
French dressing
salt and pepper

Cook the fiddleheads in lightly salted water until slightly tender. Drain and chill in ice.

Place the fiddleheads in a glass dish. Cover with the onion rings, cucumber slices and French dressing. Allow to chill for 3 hours before serving. Season with salt and pepper.

Serves 6   THE NATURAL WORLD COOKBOOK
                                                              Joe Freitus

Cooked eggplant marinated in a garlic-herb dressing.

Balkan Eggplant Salad

1 eggplant
1 tablespoon sugar
1 teaspoon salt
1 clove garlic, mashed
¼ cup vegetable or olive oil
½ cup cider vinegar
½ teaspoon fresh or dried basil
½ teaspoon fresh or dried oregano
½ teaspoon freshly ground black pepper

Wash the eggplant, leaving the skin on, and cut into 2-inch squares. Then cook 15 minutes in a small amount of boiling water until crisp-tender; drain and set aside. On a shallow plate mash the garlic with the sugar and the salt. Add the oil and let stand for 5 minutes. Scrape this mixture off into a large bowl; add the vinegar and herbs and mix thoroughly. Add the drained eggplant pieces. Chill the salad in a covered bowl, stirring occasionally so that all the eggplant is saturated with the dressing.

Serves 6–8   FRESH VEGETABLES COOKBOOK
                              Eden Gray and Mary Beckwith Cohen

A crisp unusual salad that's good with fried shrimp, chicken, or pork.

Japanese Salad

2 small heads of iceberg lettuce, or 1 very large
½ cup red apple, sliced thin (or pomegranate seeds or carrot
      shavings)
3 tablespoons frozen concentrated orange juice
2 tablespoons lemon juice
1 tablespoon cider vinegar
1 teaspoon raw egg yolk
2 tablespoons sugar
½ cup salad oil
½ teaspoon salt

Remove several layers of the green outside lettuce leaves, as the pale inside leaves are the crispest. (You may use these large outer leaves as lettuce cups.) With a large, very sharp knife, slice the head of lettuce crossways, as thinly as possible. Refrigerate the lettuce in a plastic bag for at least an hour to crisp.

Briskly stir together all the remaining ingredients except the apple to make the dressing. When ready to serve, toss the lettuce and apple with the dressing. Serve in a large bowl or mound in individual lettuce cups.

Serves 5–6   SALADS
                                                    Suzanne Best

Colorful chopped vegetables and a ricotta-mustard-yogurt dressing add zest to tasty whole-wheat pasta.

Whole Wheat Macaroni Salad

¼ pound whole wheat macaroni
¼ cup sliced or chopped ripe olives
1 bell pepper, chopped coarsely
1 tablespoon chopped parsley
½ teaspoon dill
½ teaspoon basil
2 scallions and tops, chopped
red pimientoes, to taste
1 cup ricotta cheese
2 teaspoons mustard
yogurt
salt and pepper

Cook whole wheat macaroni according to directions on package until al dente. Do not overcook. Drain and chill.

Add olives, pepper, parsley, dill and basil. Add chopped scallions, pimientoes. Toss well.

Mix ricotta cheese and mustard. Thin with yogurt to a mayonnaise-like consistency. Add salt and pepper to taste, Mix well into salad. Serve on a bed of lettuce.

Serves 4   YOUR HEALTH UNDER SIEGE
Jeffrey Bland

An attractive and tasty combination.

Watercress and Sprout Salad

1½ cups mung bean sprouts
1 bunch watercress
1 tablespoon minced chives
2 tablespoons salad oil
1 tablespoon vinegar
1 tablespoon soy sauce
1 teaspoon sugar

Combine sprouts, watercress and chives. Chill in refrigerator for a few hours.

In small bowl mix oil, vinegar, soy sauce, and sugar. Just before serving pour dressing over sprout-watercress mixture.

Serves 2–3   SPROUTS TO GROW AND EAT
                                      Esther Munroe

Cooked spinach is chilled and dressed with sour cream, lemon juice, mint and minced onion.

Persian Spinach Salad

1 package (10-ounces) fresh spinach, or ¾ pound loose
½ cup sour cream
1 tablespoon lemon juice
2 teaspoons crumbled dried mint
1 tablespoon minced onion
½ teaspoon salt
¼ teaspoon freshly ground black pepper

Thoroughly wash the spinach, break off any discolored leaves and the large, thick stems. Shake off the water and place the spinach in a very large tightly covered saucepan. Cook over medium-low heat about 10 minutes, stirring once or twice. The few drops of water that cling to the leaves will provide sufficient moisture.

When the cooked spinach has cooled, chop it very fine and place it in a bowl; add the other ingredients and mix well. Chill for an hour and bring your Persian salad to the table in a pretty bowl.

Serves 3–4   SALADS
                                                      Suzanne Best

A delicious Middle Eastern salad made from bulghur, tomatoes, scallions and lots of chopped parsley and chopped mint. This version includes beans in the mixture.

Tabouli: A Lebanese Salad

¾ cup cooked or canned white or garbanzo beans
1¼ cups bulghur wheat, raw
1½ cups fresh parsley, minced
¾ cup fresh mint, minced (if not available, substitute more
    parsley)
¾ cup scallions, chopped
3 medium tomatoes, chopped
½ cup (or more) lemon juice
¼ cup olive oil
1–2 teaspoons freshly ground pepper, to taste

Pour 4 cups boiling water over bulghur wheat. Let stand covered about 2 hours until light and fluffy. Remove excess water by shaking in a strainer or squeezing with hands.

Combine cooked, squeezed bulghur with beans, parsley, mint, scallions, tomatoes. Add lemon juice and olive oil. Season with pepper to taste.

Chill for at least 1 hour.

Serve on raw grape, lettuce, or cabbage leaves.

Serves 6   Your Health Under Siege
                                                      Jeffrey Bland

Apple, celery, and chutney make a refreshing molded salad. Try it with pork.

Chutney Salad Mold

1½ cups canned apple juice
1 tablespoon plain gelatin
½ cup chutney relish
½ cup diced celery
1 medium apple, peeled and diced
1 tablespoon diced canned pimiento

Combine ½ cup of the apple juice with the gelatin and let stand 5 minutes. Place over low heat and stir until gelatin is dissolved. Remove from heat and add remaining apple juice. Cool and chill until partially set. Add chutney, apple, celery, and pimiento. Pour into individual molds and chill until firm.

Serves 6   REAL, OLD-TIME YANKEE APPLE COOKING
Beatrice Vaughan

Goes well with vegetable salads. Wine vinegars can be substituted for the lemon juice.

Blue Cheese-Yogurt Dressing

3–4 ounces blue cheese
1 clove garlic, crushed
½ cup olive oil or salad oil
¼ cup lemon juice
1 cup plain mature yogurt
¼ teaspoon thyme
Salt and freshly ground pepper to taste
Optional: dash cayenne

Mash cheese with garlic in small bowl. Gradually stir in oil and beat until thoroughly mixed. Add lemon juice, yogurt and seasonings, mixing well. Cover and chill at least 2 hours.

Makes about 1¾ cups

THE COOK'S ADVISOR
Camille J. Stagg

Especially good on fruit. Nice on chicken, tuna, or vegetable salads, too.

Orange-Poppyseed-Yogurt Dressing

1 cup plain thin or mature yogurt
2 tablespoons orange juice
1 tablespoon lemon juice
1 teaspoon poppyseeds
Optional: 1 tablespoon honey

Blend all ingredients in small bowl or container. Honey can be added when dressing is intended for fruit salad. Cover and chill at least 2 hours.

Makes about 1¼ cups

THE COOK'S ADVISOR
Camille J. Stagg

Anchovies give this dressing its character. Serve on crisp greens.

Green Goddess

½ cup sour cream
½ cup mayonnaise
½ cup minced fresh parsley
½ cup minced scallions (or 3 tablespoons minced onion)
10 anchovy fillets, mashed
3 tablespoons lemon juice
3 tablespoons wine vinegar
¼ teaspoon dried tarragon
1 teaspoon salt
a fresh grating of pepper

Combine and stir well.

Yield: 2 cups

SALADS
Suzanne Best

Stored in brine for three weeks, lemons retain their color and shape but lose their bitterness. They make an interesting garnish for vegetable salads.

Pickled Lemons

6 lemons
1 quart water
¾ cup salt

Score each lemon with a deep cross and pile them in a covered jar. Heat the salt and water in a saucepan and stir until the salt dissolves. Pour this brine over the lemons until they are submerged. Cover tightly, refrigerate and forget them for 3 weeks. If you leave the unused lemons in the brine you can enjoy them for a month or even two.

SALADS
Suzanne Best

Breads

An unusual bread made with whole wheat flour and cider, mildly spiced — dark and nutritious.

Apple Cider Bread

2 packets dry yeast (or 2 yeast cakes)
3 cups apple cider
½ cup oil
¼ cup honey
1 tablespoon salt
1 tablespoon nutmeg
2 tablespoons cinnamon
about 7 cups whole wheat flour

Dissolve yeast in ½ cup of the cider heated to lukewarm. Warm the remaining cider and add yeast, oil, honey, salt, nutmeg, cinnamon, and 2 cups of the flour. Beat 2 minutes on the medium speed of an electric mixer. Add 2 more cups of flour and beat at high speed for 2 minutes.

Stir in enough more flour to make a dough, turn onto a board and knead until smooth and elastic, about 7 to 10 minutes. Shape into a ball and place in a greased bowl, turning to coat all sides. Cover and let rise in a warm place until double in bulk, about 1½ hours.

Punch dough down and divide in half. Cover and let rest 5 minutes. Shape into 2 loaves and place in greased 8½ × 4½-inch bread pans. Cover and let rise in a warm place until double.

Bake in a preheated 375° F oven about 50 minutes, or until loaves sound hollow when tapped on the bottom. Cover pans with aluminum foil the last 20 minutes of baking to avoid excess browning.

Yield: 2 loaves   BASIC BREADS AROUND THE WORLD
                                     Beverly Kees

Bagels are wonderful with any soft cheese and are a special treat with cream cheese and smoked salmon.

Bagels

1 cup scalded milk
¼ cup butter
1½ tablespoons sugar
½ teaspoon salt
1 packet dry yeast (or 1 yeast cake)
1 egg, separated
3¾ cups unbleached white or all-purpose flour

Combine milk, butter, sugar and salt. Cool to lukewarm. Dissolve yeast in milk mixture, then add egg white beaten but not stiff, and flour. Turn out on a floured board and knead until smooth and elastic, about 5 minutes. Shape into a ball and place in greased bowl, turning to coat all sides. Cover and let rise until double in bulk, about 1½ hours. Punch dough down and divide into 24 pieces. With floured hands, start to roll each piece into a ½-inch-thick roll, completing rolling on a board. Shape rope into a ring, overlapping ends slightly and pressing firmly to seal. Cover and let rise until not quite double in bulk.

Drop rings into hot but not boiling water until rings hold their shape, no more than 30 seconds on each side. Place rings on greased baking sheets. Whisk the separated egg yolk with 2 tablespoons water, brush tops to glaze. Bake in a preheated 400° F oven for 25 to 30 minutes, or until golden brown.

Yield: 24 bagels   BASIC BREADS AROUND THE WORLD
Beverly Kees

A dark rich loaf which uses white and medium rye flour.

Black Bread

½ cup cornmeal
½ cup cold water
1 cup boiling water
1 tablespoon shortening
1 tablespoon salt
2 tablespoons brown sugar
1½ teaspoons caraway seeds
1 ounce unsweetened chocolate, melted
1 tablespoon instant coffee
2 packets dry yeast (or 2 yeast cakes)
¾ cup lukewarm water
3 cups medium rye flour
about 3 cups unbleached white or all-purpose flour
1 egg white beaten with 1 tablespoon water, room temperature

Combine cornmeal and cold water and stir; add boiling water and stir a few minutes more. Add shortening, salt, brown sugar, caraway seeds, chocolate, and instant coffee; cool to lukewarm.

Meanwhile dissolve yeast in the ¾ cup lukewarm water for 5 minutes; add to the cornmeal mixture. Beat in rye flour, then enough white flour to make a dough. Turn out onto a floured board and knead until elastic, about 10 minutes. Shape into a ball and place in a greased bowl, turning to coat all sides. Cover and let rise in a warm place until double in bulk, about 2 to 2½ hours.

Punch dough down and knead a couple of minutes. Divide dough in half, cover and let rise 5 minutes. Shape into round balls and place on greased 8-inch pie tins. Cover and let rise until doubled.

Paint tops with egg-white-and-water glaze and bake in pre-heated 375° F oven for 50 minutes, or until loaves sound hollow when tapped on the bottom.

Yield: 2 loaves　　　　　　BASIC BREADS AROUND THE WORLD
Beverly Kees

Easy to make, this bread goes well with omelets or scrambled eggs.

Cheese-Onion Bread

½ cup diced onion
2 tablespoons butter or margarine
1½ cups packaged biscuit mix
1 cup shredded store (Cheddar) cheese (¼ pound)
1 egg, beaten
½ cup milk

Simmer the onion in 1 tablespoon of the melted butter until tender and golden. Combine the biscuit mix with ⅔ cup of the cheese; add beaten egg and milk, mixing just enough to wet all ingredients; stir in the onion.

Spread in well-greased 8-inch cake pan, brush top with re-maining melted butter, then scatter remaining cheese over all. Bake in 400° F oven for about 20 minutes and serve at once.

Serves 4–6　　　　　　STORE-CHEESE COOKING
Beatrice Vaughan

Carrots and raisins add moisture and flavor to this lightly spiced zesty loaf. Try it toasted.

Old-fashioned Orange-Carrot Bread

2 envelopes dry yeast
1 cup lukewarm water
¼ cup sugar
1 tablespoon salt
½ teaspoon cinnamon
¼ teaspoon nutmeg
¼ teaspoon allspice
1 beaten egg
¼ cup melted shortening
⅔ cup lukewarm fresh orange juice
2 tablespoons grated orange rind
about 6 cups sifted flour
1½ cups golden raisins
1½ cups grated raw carrots

Soften yeast in the warm water. Add the sugar, salt, and spices. Add beaten egg and shortening, then add orange juice and grated rind. Stir in 3 cups of the flour and beat until smooth. Add raisins and grated carrots. Stir in remaining flour to make a firm yet soft dough. Knead until smooth. Cover and let rise until doubled.

Knead again, then shape into 2 loaves. Place in greased tins, cover and let rise again until doubled. Bake at 375° F for about 50 minutes, or until bread tests done. Turn out on wire rack and brush tops with melted butter. Cool well before slicing.

Yield: 2 loaves

CITRUS COOKING
Beatrice Vaughan

A cross between corn muffins and rolls, raised with yeast for lightness and rolled out for cutting with a biscuit cutter. An heirloom recipe.

Cornmeal Raised Rolls

2 cups milk
½ cup cornmeal
⅓ cup sugar
½ cup butter
1 egg, beaten
1 teaspoon salt
1 yeast cake (or envelope)
¼ cup lukewarm water
about 3½ cups flour

Scald milk and add cornmeal, cook for about 5 minutes, stirring constantly. Remove from heat and add sugar and butter. Cool, then add beaten egg, salt and yeast, which has been dissolved in ¼ cup lukewarm water. Add flour, using a little more if needed to make a rather soft dough. Cover and let rise in a warm place until doubled in bulk.

Turn out on a floured board and knead until smooth. Roll dough out to about ⅓ inch thick and cut into rounds with biscuit cutter. Place in greased baking pan (8 × 15), cover with a towel and let rise until doubled. Bake in 425° F oven for about 15 minutes.

Yield: 30–36 rolls   YANKEE HILL-COUNTRY COOKING
                                              Beatrice Vaughan

Nice served with a hearty soup.

Pepper Cheese Bread

2 tablespoons shortening
2 tablespoons sugar
1 teaspoon salt
¾ cup milk, scalded
1 yeast cake
¼ cup lukewarm water
1 egg, beaten
about 3 cups sifted flour
1 teaspoon pepper (yes!)
1 cup shredded store (Cheddar) cheese

Add shortening, sugar and salt to the hot milk and stir until shortening is melted. Cool to lukewarm, then add the yeast, which has been softened in the lukewarm water. Stir in beaten egg, then add the flour, which has been sifted with the teaspoon of pepper. Knead to make smooth, firm dough. Cover and let rise in warm place until doubled.

Knead again, sprinkling cheese over and kneading in. Shape into long loaf and place on greased baking pan. Cover and let rise until doubled.

Bake in a 375° F oven for about 40 minutes. Brush top and sides with melted butter and cool.

Makes 1 loaf   THE OLD COOK'S ALMANAC
                                            Beatrice Vaughan

Pizza dough from scratch is not hard, and once you've learned how to make the shell, you can explore a whole world of creative combinations for toppings.

Basic Dough for Pizza

1 package active dry yeast
1 cup warm water (105°–115° F)
3 cups flour (about)
1 teaspoon sugar
½ teaspoon salt
2 tablespoons olive oil
1 tablespoon cornmeal (optional)

Soften yeast in warm water. Mix in 1½ cups flour; add sugar, salt, oil, and the rest of the flour. Knead until smooth and elastic. Grease bowl, place dough inside, then grease dough surface and cover with cloth. Let rise in a warm place, about 85° F, until double in bulk — about 1½ hours.

Punch down, roll out on floured surface to fit two 13-inch round pie pans (sprinkle pans with cornmeal before baking). Push the sides of the dough up about half an inch to hold filling. The dough is now ready to be filled and baked at 450° F for 15–20 minutes, or until the crust is a golden brown.

Makes two 12-inch pies   PIZZA: THEME AND VARIATIONS
Rita Blinderman

Ground lamb or beef and vegetables top these individual pizzas.

Armenian Pizza
(Lahmejoun or Missahatz)

1 prepared recipe Basic Dough
1 pound ground lamb or beef
½ cup chopped green pepper
¾ cup chopped parsley
1 chopped garlic clove
½ cup chopped onion
1 teaspoon paprika with a bit of cayenne
½ teaspoon allspice
salt and pepper to taste
1½ cups chopped plum tomatoes
2 tablespoons tomato paste

Divide dough into eight equal portions. Form into balls, set on lightly-floured board, and cover with plastic wrap or damp tea towel.

Wait 15 minutes, then roll each ball out to an 8-inch circle. Place on greased baking sheets. Combine meat, tomatoes and seasonings; spread equal portions of mixture over surface of each circle.

Bake on bottom shelf of oven, preheated to 500° F, from 6 to 9 minutes until bottom of dough changes color. Remove baking sheet to top shelf and continue to cook about 5 minutes. Do not overcook. Serve hot or cold.

Makes 8 small pies   PIZZA: THEME AND VARIATIONS
                                          Rita Blinderman

Refried beans, tomato sauce, and meat are garnished with lettuce, onion, and avocado.

Mexican Pizza Sombrero

¾ pound chopped meat
1 cup tomato sauce
1 peeled chopped tomato
1 teaspoon chili powder
½ teaspoon cumin powder
½ teaspoon garlic powder
½ teaspoon salt
1 teaspoon sugar
1 tablespoon lemon juice
1 15½-ounce can refried beans
1 cup Cheddar cheese
¼ cup canned California chilies, chopped
1 avocado, thinly sliced
   Basic dough recipe made with 3 tablespoons yellow cornmeal in place of 3 tablespoons of the flour

Prepare pizza shell for 12-inch pie. Grease pie pan, sprinkle with additional cornmeal. Spread dough over this. Shape pie shell with ½-inch lip at edges.

  Brown meat; drain liquid. Mix tomato sauce with spices and lemon juice; and to meat. Simmer, uncovered, 15 minutes. Spread a layer of refried beans over dough, then a layer of meat and sauce. Top with cheese. Scatter chilies over surface. Bake in 450° F oven, on bottom shelf, 15 to 20 minutes, or until crust turns golden brown. Serve hot with a helping of lettuce, onion, avocado on top.

Makes 4–6 slices   PIZZA: THEME AND VARIATIONS
Rita Blinderman

An interesting variation.

Pizza Ratatouille

1 onion, chopped
1 garlic clove, minced
¼ cup olive oil
1 small eggplant, diced
1 medium zucchini, diced
½ green pepper, diced
1 small can tomato sauce
1 teaspoon oregano
1 teaspoon basil
salt and pepper to taste
¼ cup Parmesan cheese
1 twelve-inch pie shell, unbaked (Basic Dough recipe)

Sauté onion and garlic in olive oil until transparent. Mix in eggplant, zucchini and green pepper and sauté for ten minutes. Blend in tomato sauce and seasonings. Cover and simmer for 30 minutes. Remove cover and cook 20 minutes more.

Spread mixture over pie shell. Sprinkle Parmesan cheese over top. Bake in 450° F oven for twenty minutes, or until pie shell turns golden brown.

Makes one 12-inch pie   PIZZA: THEME AND VARIATIONS
Rita Blinderman

This flat bread with a pocket is excellent stuffed with salad or sandwich fillings.

Middle East Pita

1 packet dry yeast (or 1 yeast cake)
1¼ cups lukewarm water
1 tablespoon oil
1 teaspoon salt
1 teaspoon sugar
about 4 cups unbleached white or all-purpose flour

Dissolve yeast in water for 5 minutes. Add oil, salt, sugar and 1 cup flour; beat well. Mix in enough flour to make a stiff dough, turn out on a floured board, and knead 10 minutes. Cover and let dough rest 5 minutes.

Divide dough into 12 pieces; shape each into a ball. Roll out each ball on a well-floured board to make a flat circle about 5 inches in diameter. Let rounds rest on heavily floured surface 30 minutes, then turn gently and let rest another 30 minutes.

Place rounds on floured baking sheets and bake in a preheated 500° F oven for about 5 minutes, turning them over after the first three minutes. The rounds will puff up and get light brown spots. Do only one or two at first to check temperature and timing.

Yield: 12 rounds   BASIC BREADS AROUND THE WORLD
Beverly Kees

No kneading required for this batter bread which has a coarser texture than conventional kneaded yeast breads.

Whole-Grain Batter Bread

1½ cups boiling water
½ cup soy, margarine, or butter
¼ cup honey
2 teaspoons kelp powder
2 packages active dry yeast
1 cup warm water
2 cups Quaker Oats (Quick or Old Fashioned)
5 to 6 cups whole wheat flour
2 eggs
1 cup chopped walnuts

Combine boiling water, margarine, honey, and kelp powder in large bowl, stirring until margarine melts. Cool to lukewarm. Dissolve yeast in warm water. (To check water temperature, test it on your wrist in the same way you would test a baby bottle. The water should be a little hotter.) Stir dissolved yeast, oats, 2 cups of flour, eggs, and nuts into lukewarm water mixture; mix well. Stir in enough of the remaining flour to make a stiff batter. Place in a large, greased bowl. Cover; let rise in warm place 1 to 1½ hours or until double in size.

   Spoon batter into two well-greased 9″ × 5″ loaf pans. Let rise uncovered in warm place 30 to 45 minutes, or until nearly double in size. Bake in preheated 375° F oven for 30 to 35 minutes or until golden brown. Cool at least 1 hour before slicing.

Yield: 2 loaves   YOUR HEALTH UNDER SIEGE
                                         Jeffrey Bland

Easy and quick to prepare. Chop walnuts finely so that the loaf will slice well.

Black Walnut Loaf

¾ cup chopped walnuts
¾ cup sugar
2 tablespoons shortening
1 egg
1 tablespoon applesauce or apple butter
3 cups flour
3½ teaspoons baking powder
1 teaspoon salt
1½ cups milk

Cream together the sugar and shortening. Stir in the egg and applesauce. Sift together the flour, baking powder, and salt. Add the milk and then the dry ingredients to the shortening mixture. Add the nut meats and stir thoroughly. Pour the batter into a greased loaf pan. Bake at 350° F for 1 hour, or until done. Serve hot and buttered.

Yield: 1 loaf

THE NATURAL WORLD COOKBOOK
Joe Freitus

These corn muffins have a tangy cheese mixture dabbed on the top. The result is lovely: the bread remains golden, the topping a pale yellow touched with brown.

Cheese-Corn Puffs

½ cup unsifted flour
2 tablespoons sugar
2 teaspoons baking powder
¼ teaspoon salt
½ cup yellow cornmeal
1 egg, separated
½ cup milk
1 tablespoon melted bacon fat
½ cup shredded sharp store (Cheddar) cheese (⅛ pound)
1 tablespoon soft butter or margarine
¼ teaspoon Worcestershire sauce

Sift flour with sugar, baking powder and salt; add cornmeal. Add egg yolk and milk to dry mixture, then the bacon fat; stir only enough to moisten all thoroughly. Fill greased 2-inch muffin cups about ½ full and bake at 425° F for 10 minutes.

While they bake, beat egg white stiff, then fold in the cheese, butter and Worcestershire sauce. Remove muffins from oven, put 1 teaspoon of cheese mixture on top of each muffin and return to oven, using top rack, until top is puffed and brown — about 5 minutes more. Serve at once.

Yield: 12 muffins

STORE-CHEESE COOKING
Beatrice Vaughan

Apples, raisins, nuts, and maple syrup make these delectable.

Maple-Apple Buns

2 cups sifted flour
1 teaspoon baking powder
½ teaspoon baking soda
1 teaspoon salt
4 tablespoons shortening
1 cup buttermilk
2 tablespoons butter or margarine
¼ cup maple syrup
2 tablespoons sugar
¼ teaspoon cinnamon
2 medium apples, peeled and thinly sliced
½ cup chopped seeded raisins
¼ cup chopped nuts

Sift flour with baking powder, soda, and salt. Rub in the shortening, then mix in the buttermilk. Knead slightly on floured
board, roll about ¼ inch thick. Spread with the softened butter.
 Mix maple syrup, sugar and cinnamon and spread over butter.
Scatter apple slices, raisins and nuts evenly over surface. Roll
lengthwise as for jelly roll and cut in slices about 1 inch thick.
Place flat on greased baking sheet. Bake in 375° F oven for about
30 minutes, or until apples are tender and crust browned.

Yield: 16 buns   REAL, OLD-TIME YANKEE MAPLE COOKING
Beatrice Vaughan

Tasty for breakfast or good with baked ham or roast pork.

Orange Filled Rolls

2 cups sifted flour
4 teaspoons baking powder
¾ teaspoon salt
1 teaspoon sugar
1 teaspoon grated orange rind
¼ cup shortening
¾ cup milk

Filling

2 tablespoons flour
1½ tablespoons melted butter
¼ cup orange juice
1 teaspoon grated orange rind
¼ cup sugar

Sift flour with baking powder, salt and sugar. Mix in orange rind, then rub in shortening. Add milk. Knead dough slightly and roll out to about ½ inch thick.

Spread with the filling and roll lengthwise as for jelly roll. Cut in 1-inch crosswise slices. Place each in greased muffin tin and bake in a 400° F oven for about 18 minutes.

To make the filling, stir flour into the melted butter, then add orange juice and rind. Cook over low heat until smooth and thick, stirring constantly. Add sugar, stir well and cool before using.

Makes 12–15   THE OLD COOK'S ALMANAC
                                        Beatrice Vaughan

A classic bread from India, this is especially appropriate with a spicy curry.

Pooris

1 cup unbleached white or all-purpose flour
1 cup whole wheat flour
2 tablespoons melted butter
½ teaspoon salt
about ½ cup water
oil for shallow frying

Combine flours and mix in the butter. Add salt and just enough water to make a stiff dough. Turn out on a lightly floured board and knead about 7 minutes. Return to bowl, cover and let rest 1 hour.

Heat about ½ inch of oil in a heavy skillet. Tear dough into 2-inch balls and roll out to ¼-inch-thick circles. Fry one at a time, turning frequently so it puffs up; frying should take about 30 to 40 seconds. Drain on paper towels and serve hot.

Yield: 10–12 pooris   BASIC BREADS AROUND THE WORLD
Beverly Kees

Maple syrup and nuts combine beautifully. Try them in muffins or in a rich, blueberry-studded bread.

Black Walnut Maple Muffins

 1 cup finely chopped walnuts
 2 cups flour
 ½ teaspoon salt
 3 teaspoons baking powder
 ¼ cup shortening
 1 egg
 ⅓ cup maple syrup
 ½ cup milk

Sift together three times the flour, salt and baking powder. Add the shortening, egg, maple syrup and milk. Mix thoroughly. Spoon the batter into a greased muffin tin. Bake at 375° F for about 20–25 minutes. Serve hot and buttered.

Yield: 12 muffins   THE NATURAL WORLD COOKBOOK
                                             Joe Freitus

Blueberry Maple Nut Bread

1 cup of ripe blueberries
2 cups flour
1 teaspoon baking soda
½ teaspoon salt
½ cup chopped nuts
⅔ cup maple syrup
¾ cup melted butter
2 beaten eggs

Sift together the flour, baking soda and salt. Add the blueberries and nut meats. Stir carefully and evenly until the blueberries and nuts are evenly coated with the flour mixture.

In a separate bowl combine the maple syrup, melted butter and 2 well-beaten eggs. Mix thoroughly with the berry mixture.

Select either a single large bread pan or 2 smaller ones. Grease the pan or line with waxed paper. Bake at 320° F for about 1 hour. Serve hot, plain or glazed.

Yield: 1–2 loaves   THE NATURAL WORLD COOKBOOK
Joe Freitus

Desserts

An unusual method that works.

Paper-Bag Apple Pie

6–7 cups peeled, sliced apples
1 cup sugar
½ cup flour plus 2 tablespoons
½ teaspoon nutmeg
unbaked 9-inch pie shell
2 tablespoons lemon juice
½ cup softened butter or margarine

Combine apple slices, ½ cup of the sugar, and 2 tablespoons of the flour; add nutmeg and toss well to mix. Turn into the pie shell and sprinkle with lemon juice.

Combine remaining ½ cup sugar with the remaining ½ cup flour, rub in the butter, and sprinkle the topping evenly over the apples. Place pie in large, heavy paper bag. Fold end over twice and fasten with paper clips. Place bag on cookie sheet. Bake in 425° F oven for 1 hour. Split bag open and remove pie to cool. Serve warm with good regional Cheddar "store" cheese.

Serves 6–8   REAL, OLD-TIME YANKEE APPLE COOKING
Beatrice Vaughan

Rich and light.

Maple Chiffon Pie

1 tablespoon plain gelatin
2 tablespoons cold water
½ cup maple syrup
½ cup milk
pinch of salt
2 eggs, separated
1 cup heavy cream
1 teaspoon vanilla
baked 9-inch pie shell
2 tablespoons finely chopped nuts

Soak gelatin in the cold water. Combine maple syrup, milk and salt and heat in the top of a double boiler. Beat egg yolks until light, then pour the hot syrup mixture over them very slowly, beating constantly. Return to heat and cook over hot water until custard is smooth and as thick as heavy cream, stirring constantly. Add the gelatin and stir until dissolved. Remove from heat and cool, then chill in refrigerator until partially thickened.

Whip cream until stiff and fold in. Fold in vanilla. Beat egg whites until stiff, and fold in. Pour into cooled pie shell and sprinkle with nuts. Keep in refrigerator for several hours, or until set.

Serves 8   REAL, OLD-TIME YANKEE MAPLE COOKING
Beatrice Vaughan

A subtle blend of flavorings.

Maple Pumpkin Pie

2 eggs
3 tablespoons light brown sugar
½ teaspoon ginger
¾ teaspoon cinnamon
pinch of salt
¾ cup maple syrup
1 cup undiluted evaporated milk
2 cups strained pumpkin (canned is fine)
unbaked 9-inch pie shell

Beat eggs well. Combine sugar, spices and salt, and beat into the eggs. Add maple syrup, evaporated milk and pumpkin, and mix all well with a rotary beater. Pour into pie shell and bake in a 450° F oven for 10 minutes. Reduce heat to 350° F and bake about 40 minutes longer, or until a knife blade comes out clean when inserted in center of pie. Serve with "store" cheese (natural Cheddar), the perfect companion.

Serves 8　　　　　　　REAL, OLD-TIME YANKEE MAPLE COOKING
Beatrice Vaughan

Apple pie with a difference.

Spicy Fruit-Nut Pie

1¼ cups sugar
½ teaspoon cinnamon
¼ teaspoon each ginger and ground cloves
pinch of salt
1½ cups finely chopped apple (2 medium)
1 cup seedless raisins
½ cup jellied cranberry sauce
½ cup chopped nuts
1 teaspoon grated orange rind
1 teaspoon grated lemon rind
¼ cup lemon juice
1 tablespoon butter or margarine
pastry for 2-crust, 9-inch pie

Combine sugar, spices, and salt, and add to chopped apple. Add raisins, cranberry sauce, and nuts. Stir in grated rinds and lemon juice; mix well, then pour into pastry-lined pie tin.

Dot with the butter, cover with top crust. Bake in 450° F oven for 10 minutes; reduce heat to 375° F and continue to bake about 40 minutes longer. Serve warm with "store" cheese (natural Cheddar).

Serves 8   Real, Old-Time Yankee Apple Cooking
Beatrice Vaughan

Ground almonds or hazelnuts take the place of flour. Filled with whipped cream this is a marvelously light confection.

Rolled Almond or Hazelnut Cake
Biscuit Roulé aux Amandes ou aux Noisettes

    salad oil
    8 egg yolks
    ¾ cup granulated sugar
    1½ cups ground almonds or hazelnuts*
    8 egg whites
    1 cup heavy cream
    1 tablespoon confectioners' sugar, sifted
    whole almonds or hazelnuts

Saturate a piece of paper towel with oil and coat a teflon or other cookie sheet that measures roughly 11 × 15 inches. Be sure the bottom, corners, and sides are all well coated. Line with waxed paper, being careful to fit it up the sides, too. Snip corners with scissors so that the paper will fit well into the corners. Oil again on top of waxed paper.

Preheat oven to 350° F.

Using a large wire whisk, beat egg yolks in a large bowl for 1 minute; then gradually beat in sugar. This will take another 4 minutes.

Next, gradually blend in ground nuts with a wooden spoon.

In a large bowl, beat egg whites with electric mixer at high speed for 2 minutes, cleaning sides of bowl several times with a rubber spatula. Then, slowly fold egg whites carefully into almond batter, a small portion at a time. Do not stir.

Pour this batter onto prepared cookie sheet, spread out evenly with a spatula; bake on middle rack of oven for 18 minutes. When done, pastry should feel firm to the touch; it will be a light golden brown.

Remove from oven, cool completely, then cover with a damp linen towel and refrigerate for a minimum of 2 hours. If keeping more than 2 hours, be sure towel stays damp, wetting it again if necessary.

Chill bowl and beaters in freezer; then whip cream for 3 minutes at high speed, using rubber spatula to clean bowl. Using a large wire whisk, fold in confectioners' sugar.

Cover a pastry board with two sheets of waxed paper, making them large enough to overlap the board at least 4 inches all the way around. Turn cake onto the board so that its underside is on top. Peel off original waxed paper.

Working with a long edge of cake near you, spread about ⅔ of the cream in a narrow line about 1 inch in from front edge, leaving an inch at both ends also, so that cream will not be squeezed out when the cake is rolled.

Starting with the front edge, roll cake, folding cream within it. It helps to roll the waxed paper with it until the cake begins to overlap. Decorate the outside with remaining cream, using a rubber spatula or pastry bag. Fill in both ends and cracks, if any.

Sprinkle the top with almonds or hazelnuts, depending upon which kind of cake was made.

Yield: 14–16 slices   My French Kitchen
                                               Denise Khaitman Schorr

*A 6-ounce cellophane bag will yield 1⅔ cups of nuts when ground. Place ¾ cup at a time in an electric blender and whirl at high speed while you count to 10. Or use a food processor.

An unusual flavor combination.

Blackberry Jam Cake

⅔ cup butter, softened
1 cup sugar
3 eggs, well beaten
1 cup blackberry jam (or raspberry jam)
¼ cup black coffee
4 tablespoons sour cream
2½ cups sifted flour
1 teaspoon baking powder
1 teaspoon baking soda
pinch of salt
1 teaspoon cinnamon
½ teaspoon ground cloves
about 2½ cups Mocha Frosting

Cream butter and sugar. Add egg and jam and beat well. Sift dry ingredients together and add to first mixture alternately with sour cream and coffee. Beat all well. Pour into 2 greased layer-cake pans and bake in a 350° F oven for about 30 minutes. Cool layers and put together with Mocha Frosting between layers and spread over top and sides.

Mocha Frosting

2 egg whites
1½ cups granulated sugar
4 tablespoons cold strong coffee
¼ teaspoon cream of tartar
1 teaspoon vanilla

Place egg whites, sugar, cream of tartar and coffee in top of double boiler and cook over boiling water, beating constantly with an egg beater until frosting will stand in peaks, 5 to 7 minutes. Remove from heat, add vanilla and beat until smooth, 1 minute more. Spread immediately on cooled cake. Will make about 2½ cups.

If an electric beater is used, the cooking time may be shorter, perhaps as little as 4 minutes.

YANKEE HILL-COUNTRY COOKING
Beatrice Vaughan

Easy, quick and good.

Poppy Seed Cake

1 box poppy seeds (2½ ounces)
1 cup milk
2 eggs
¾ cup oil
¾ cup honey
½ teaspoon vanilla or almond extract
2 cups whole wheat flour
¼ cup instant milk powder
dash cinnamon and/or nutmeg
2½ teaspoons baking powder

Soak poppy seeds in milk for 1 hour in a large bowl.

Add eggs, oil, honey, and vanilla or almond extract to poppy seed mixture. Beat together.

Mix flour, milk powder, cinnamon and/or nutmeg and baking powder. Add dry ingredients to wet ones and mix.

Bake in a greased and floured cake pan at 350° F for 45 minutes.

YOUR HEALTH UNDER SIEGE
Jeffrey Bland

A delicious layer cake from an old hill-country recipe.

Filled Prune Cake

¾ cup butter
1 cup sugar
1 cup mashed cooked prunes (½ pound dried)
1¼ cups flour
1 teaspoon baking soda
1 teaspoon cinnamon
½ teaspoon nutmeg
½ teaspoon cloves
3 tablespoons sour cream
3 eggs, beaten
1½ cups Raisin-Nut Filling
2 cups Seven-Minute White Frosting

Cream butter and sugar, add prunes, which should be well drained. Sift dry ingredients together and add to prune mixture with sour cream and beaten eggs. Blend well and bake in 2 greased layer-cake pans in a 350° F oven for about 30 minutes. Cool layers and put together with filling, and frost.

Raisin-Nut Filling

1 beaten egg
½ cup sugar
½ cup sour cream
½ cup chopped nutmeats
1 cup chopped seeded raisins

Mix all together and cook over hot water until thick, about 5 minutes, stirring constantly. Cool and spread between layers. Makes about 1½ cups.

Seven-Minute White Frosting

1½ cups sugar
4 tablespoons water
¼ teaspoon cream of tartar
2 egg whites, unbeaten
1 teaspoon vanilla

Place sugar, water, cream of tartar and egg whites in top of double boiler. Cook over boiling water until thick and smooth, beating constantly with egg beater. When frosting is stiff enough to stand in peaks, remove from heat, add vanilla and beat until smooth, 1 minute more. Spread it at once on cake before frosting cools.

If an electric beater is used, cooking time will be a little shortened, to about 5 or 6 minutes.

Makes about 2 cups   YANKEE HILL-COUNTRY COOKING
                                        Beatrice Vaughan

An old-time recipe sometimes known as "Poor Man's Fruitcake." Tasty.

Salt Pork Cake

½ pound salt pork, finely ground or diced small
1 cup brown sugar, firmly packed
1 cup molasses
1 cup boiling water
2 beaten eggs (optional)
about 5 cups flour
1 teaspoon baking soda
1 teaspoon cream of tartar
¼ teaspoon ground cloves
½ teaspoon ground cinnamon
⅛ teaspoon ground nutmeg
2 cups seeded raisins, chopped
½ cup finely chopped candied citron — about ¼ pound
     (optional)
½ cup dried currants (optional)
1 cup broken nutmeats (optional)

In a large bowl mix the salt pork well with the brown sugar, then add the molasses and the boiling water. Stir together and add the beaten eggs at this time (if you use them).

Sift together about 4 cups of the flour, the baking soda, cream of tartar and spices, and mix these dry ingredients in well with the pork mixture, a little at a time.

In a separate bowl, toss ½ cup of the remaining flour together with the raisins and optional fruits and nutmeats until they are well coated; add them to the batter, using a little flour if needed — the batter should be stiff. Spoon the batter 2½ inches deep into a 10-inch greased tube pan lined with cut-to-shape greased wax paper; put the surplus in a similarly prepared 4½ × 8-inch loaf pan (either size will yield a 2½ pound cake).

Bake the cakes in a preheated slow oven (275° F) until a tooth-pick pushed into the center of each comes out clean — about 2½ to 3 hours. Place a shallow pan of water in the oven during the first 2 hours of baking to keep the cakes from drying. Cool the cakes in their pans on a wire rack for 20 to 30 minutes, then remove the cakes and peel off their paper liners to finish the cooling. Wrap thoroughly cooled cakes securely in aluminum foil and store them in a cool, dry, safe place for at least 2 weeks before cutting.

PUTTING FOOD BY
Ruth Hertzberg, Beatrice Vaughan, Janet Greene

Variation: Wrap the cooled cakes in brandy-soaked cheesecloth and overwrap well with foil; then store in an earthenware crock in a cool place for at least 2 weeks before cutting.

Blueberries add color and flavor to this apple crisp variation.

Apple-Blueberry Crisp

2 cups blueberries
2 cups peeled, sliced apples
about ½ cup light brown sugar
⅔ cup sifted flour
½ cup sugar
1 teaspoon baking powder
½ teaspoon salt
1 egg, beaten
3 tablespoons butter or margarine, melted
cinnamon for topping.

Combine blueberries and apple slices, place in buttered baking dish and sprinkle with brown sugar, using a bit more or less according to the tartness of the fruit.

Sift together the flour, sugar, baking powder and salt. Add the beaten egg, stirring until all is in coarse crumbs; sprinkle evenly over the fruit.

Drizzle the melted butter over the top and sprinkle lightly with cinnamon. Bake about 35 minutes in a 375° F oven, or until top is crusty and the apples tender. Serve warm with cream or any whipped topping.

Serves 6   REAL, OLD-TIME YANKEE APPLE COOKING
                                          Beatrice Vaughan

Lovely topped with applesauce or confectioners' sugar.

Apple-Maple Dessert Griddlecakes

1½ cups sifted flour
3 teaspoons baking powder
½ teaspoon salt
¼ teaspoon cinnamon
¾ cup milk
¼ cup maple syrup
1 egg, beaten
3 tablespoons melted shortening
1 large apple, peeled and finely chopped

Sift flour with baking powder, salt and cinnamon. Combine milk and maple syrup; add to dry ingredients. Add beaten egg and melted shortening, then stir in the apple.

Drop by rounded tablespoonfuls onto hot, greased griddle. Bake until top is bubbly and underside golden brown; then turn, brown other side. Serve hot with confectioners' sugar sifted lightly over each cake, or top with warm, spicy applesauce.

Makes about 16 cakes

REAL, OLD-TIME YANKEE APPLE COOKING
Beatrice Vaughan

Cinnamon sauce accents this rhubarb treat.

Rhubarb Puffs with Cinnamon Sauce

1½ cups diced rhubarb
1½ cups sugar
1 cup sifted cake flour
1½ teaspoons baking powder
pinch of salt
¼ cup softened shortening
1 egg, beaten
⅓ cup milk
½ teaspoon vanilla

Sauce

¼ cup sugar
2 teaspoons flour
pinch of salt
¼ teaspoon cinnamon
¾ cup water
1 teaspoon butter

Combine rhubarb and 1 cup of the sugar. Fill muffin cups about half full. Sift flour with salt and baking powder. Cream shortening with remaining ½ cup sugar, then blend in beaten egg and vanilla. Add milk alternately with the flour mixture. Beat thoroughly, then pour batter in on top of rhubarb and sugar. Bake in a 375° F oven until puffs are brown, about 30 minutes.

Serve warm with the sauce, which has been made by combining sugar with the flour, salt and cinnamon, then adding the water. Simmer until smooth and thick, stirring constantly, then add butter. Serve hot over the warm puffs.

Makes about 12 puffs   THE OLD COOK'S ALMANAC
                                          Beatrice Vaughan

Easy and delicious.

Maple Mousse

3 egg yolks
1 cup maple syrup
4 cups whipping cream
½ teaspoon vanilla

Heat maple syrup until just below the boiling point. Beat egg
yolks until light, then add hot syrup gradually, stirring constantly. Set aside to cool. Whip cream stiff and fold into cooled
egg-and-syrup mixture. Add vanilla. Pour into 1-gallon can that
has a lid. Cover tightly and pack can in ice and rock salt to cover.
Let stand 3 hours.

Makes about 2 quarts   YANKEE HILL-COUNTRY COOKING
Beatrice Vaughan

A hand ice-cream freezer is good for this purpose because the dasher can be
removed and the hole at the top covered to keep out any salt or water. This
mousse can also be frozen in the ice-cube trays in the freezing compartment of
your refrigerator and will be quite as creamy.

If necessary, the mousse can be placed in a covered metal can in the deep
freeze, but you will need to take it out well in advance of serving time, or it will
be too hard to serve.

Serve hot with maple syrup.

Apple Fritters

1 cup sifted flour
1 teaspoon baking powder
¼ teaspoon salt
¼ teaspoon cinnamon
⅓ cup milk
2 beaten eggs
1½ cups chopped apple (about 2 medium)
fat for frying

Sift flour with baking powder, salt, and cinnamon. Combine milk and beaten eggs. Beat the 2 mixtures together well, then stir in chopped apple.

Drop by tablespoon into deep hot fat as for doughnuts. Drain on paper towel. Serve very hot with maple syrup.

Makes about 15   REAL, OLD-TIME YANKEE APPLE COOKING
Beatrice Vaughan

Preserves

Blue plums and light rum in a flavorful jam.

Plum-Rum Jam

3½ cups prepared plums
1 cup water
½ cup fresh lemon juice
7½ cups sugar
½ bottle liquid fruit pectin (3 ounces)
¼ cup light rum

Prepare plums by pitting unpeeled blue plums, then cutting into eighths. Add water and set over moderate heat. Bring to boiling, then simmer about 10 minutes, crushing plums with spoon.

Add lemon juice and sugar. Bring to a full rolling boil, stirring constantly, then cook 1 minute. Remove from heat and stir in the pectin. Stir 2 minutes, then stir in the rum. Stir 1 minute longer, then seal in hot sterilized glasses.

Makes about 4 pints   JAMS, JELLIES & MARMALADES
                                                    Beatrice Vaughan

Combines wonderfully with cream cheese for a sandwich or with crackers as an hors d'oeuvre.

Red Pepper Jam

12 sweet red peppers, seeded
1 tablespoon salt
2 cups vinegar
2 cups sugar

Grind the peppers, using medium knife. Add the salt and let stand overnight. Drain well, then combine with the vinegar and sugar. Set over moderate heat and bring to boiling, stirring constantly. Reduce heat and simmer until thick as any jam, stirring frequently. Seal in hot sterilized jars.

Makes about 2 pints   JAMS, JELLIES & MARMALADES
Beatrice Vaughan

Chopped candied ginger, lemon and oranges combine beautifully in this marmalade.

Old-Fashioned Ginger Marmalade

1 lemon
about 8 medium oranges
1½ quarts water
sugar
2 cups finely chopped candied ginger

Slice lemon paper-thin and place in a 1-quart measure. Cut enough oranges in paper-thin slices to fill the measure. Combine with the water and let stand overnight. Do not drain.

Place over moderate heat and cover. Bring to boiling, then reduce heat and simmer until peel is very tender, about 2 hours. Measure fruit and liquid and add ¾ as much sugar. Add the ginger and bring to boiling, uncovered. Stir frequently. Boil rapidly until jelly stage is reached — 220° F on jelly thermometer, or when mixture sheets from the spoon. Remove from heat and seal in hot sterilized jars.

Makes about 5 pints   JAMS, JELLIES & MARMALADES
                                              Beatrice Vaughan

Strips of grapefruit peel sugared and spiced.

Spiced Grapefruit Peel Preserves

2 large grapefruit
⅓ cup vinegar
¾ cup water
1½ cups sugar
1 large stick whole cinnamon
8 whole cloves
½ teaspoon ground ginger
pinch of salt

Peel the grapefruit, scraping the white inner membrane from the peel. Cover peel with water and bring to boil. Drain and cover with fresh water; bring again to a boil and simmer until tender, about 20 minutes. Drain. Cut the peel in thin strips, about ½ × 2 inches.

In a good-sized heavy pan, combine vinegar, water, sugar, spices and salt. Bring to a boil, stirring constantly. Add the drained peel and simmer until the syrup has thickened — about 45 minutes — stirring occasionally. Seal in hot sterilized jars.

Makes about 1½ pints   PICKLES, RELISHES & PRESERVES
                                            Beatrice Vaughan

Wonderful and different.

Spicy Cranberry-Ginger Relish

4 cups fresh cranberries
2 cups firmly packed light brown sugar
1 cup golden raisins
1 cup water
¼ cup finely chopped candied ginger
⅓ cup chopped nuts
¼ cup fresh lemon juice
1½ teaspoons salt
2 teaspoons grated onion
¼ teaspoon ground cloves

In a good-sized saucepan, combine all ingredients in order; place over moderate heat and bring to boiling. Reduce heat and simmer 15 minutes, stirring constantly. Seal in hot sterilized jars.

Makes about 2½ pints   PICKLES, RELISHES & PRESERVES
Beatrice Vaughan

Tomatoes, pears, peaches, onions, and peppers blend in this relish.

Tomato-Fruit Relish

8 pounds ripe tomatoes (about 20 large)
8 pears, peeled and cored
8 peaches, peeled and pitted
6 large onions, peeled
2 large sweet red peppers, seeded
3 cups vinegar
4 cups sugar
2 tablespoons salt
3 tablespoons mixed pickling spices

Peel the tomatoes and chop coarsely. Put pears, peaches, onions and red peppers through the food grinder, using a coarse knife.

Combine fruits and vegetables in a large enamelware kettle. Add vinegar, sugar, and salt; tie spices in a small cloth bag and add. Set over moderate heat and bring to boiling. Reduce heat and simmer until thick, about 2 hours, stirring frequently.

Remove the spice bag and pour into hot, sterilized jars. Seal jars and process in hot water bath for 5 minutes.

Makes 8 pints

PICKLES, RELISHES & PRESERVES
Beatrice Vaughan

A nice change from tomato ketchup. Good with meatloaf or pot roast.

Cape Cod Cranberry Ketchup

4 pounds fresh cranberries
1½ cups water
1½ cups vinegar
4 cups light brown sugar
1 teaspoon ground cloves
2 teaspoons ground cinnamon
1 teaspoon paprika
1 teaspoon salt

Combine cranberries, water and vinegar in a good heavy kettle. Cover and cook over low heat until the cranberries are very soft. Strain the berries and rub them through a coarse sieve.

Return to the kettle, add remaining ingredients and simmer until thick — about 45 minutes. The ketchup should be a little thinner than ordinary catsup since it thickens as it cools. Stir frequently.

Seal in hot sterilized jars.

Makes about 5 pints

PICKLES, RELISHES & PRESERVES
Beatrice Vaughan

A striking and tangy garnish for holiday roasts.

Pickled Orange Slices

12 large oranges
 7 cups sugar
 2 cups vinegar
 2 sticks whole cinnamon
 1 tablespoon whole cloves

Wash oranges, then cut in ¼-inch slices, discarding seeds. Cover slices with water and simmer for 30 minutes. Drain.

Boil sugar, vinegar and spices together for 5 minutes. Add half the amount of orange slices to the simmering syrup and cook very slowly until slices are clear. Remove from syrup, then cook remaining slices the same way.

Combine all slices with the syrup and set aside for 24 hours.

Drain syrup and cook for 10 minutes. Add slices and bring to boiling point. Pack slices in hot jars. Strain syrup and pour over slices and seal.

Makes about 6 pints   THE OLD COOK'S ALMANAC
                                                    Beatrice Vaughan

This chutney, made with easy-to-find ingredients, improves with age.

Indian Chutney

juice, pulp and peel of 1 lemon, finely chopped
2 cups cider vinegar
2½ cups dark brown sugar (1 pound)
1 clove garlic, minced
pinch of cayenne pepper (⅛ teaspoon)
pinch of chili powder (⅛ teaspoon)
1½ teaspoons salt
5½ cups coarsely chopped firm apples, peeled and cored
    (about 3 pounds), or peaches or pears
¾ cup crystallized ginger, cut small but not minced (about
    3 ounces)
1½ cups raisins, preferably seeded (½ pound)

Chop the lemon, removing seeds and saving the juice (a blender is good here), and put it in an open, heavy enameled kettle with the sugar, vinegar, minced garlic, salt, cayenne pepper and chili powder. Boil the mixture over medium heat for 30 minutes, stirring occasionally.

Meanwhile prepare the apples (or peaches or pears), and add them to the syrup with the raisins and ginger. Boil all slowly, stirring to prevent sticking and scorching, until the fruit is tender but not mushy and the syrup is thick — about 30 to 45 minutes longer.

Ladle the boiling-hot chutney into sterilized pint or ½ pint jars, filling to ⅛ inch of the top, and cap each jar immediately with a sterilized 2-piece screwband lid. Cool topside up and store.

Makes 3 pints or six ½ pints

PUTTING FOOD BY
Ruth Hertzberg, Beatrice Vaughan, Janet Greene

Acknowledgments

We gratefully acknowledge the kindness of the following authors or their heirs in allowing their recipes to be reprinted in this cookbook. The order of ingredients and some recipe formats were changed slightly in some recipes for consistency. The following authors contributed to this book:

Suzanne Best, *Salads,* © 1971 by Suzanne Best

Jeffrey Bland, *Your Health Under Siege,* © 1981 by Jeffrey Bland

Rita Blinderman, *Pizza: Theme and Variations,* © 1979 by Rita Blinderman

Beatrice Ross Buszek, *The Cranberry Connection,* © 1977, 1978 by Beatrice Ross Buszek

Adele G. Dawson, *Health, Happiness and the Pursuit of Herbs,* © 1980 by Adele Dawson

Audrey Alley Gorton, *The Venison Book,* © 1957 by The Stephen Greene Press

Eden Gray and Mary Beckwith Cohen, *The Harvest Home Fresh Vegetables Cookbook,* © 1972 by Eden Gray and Mary Beckwith Cohen

Marjorie Hamilton, *The Harvest Home Hors D'Oeuvres Book,* © 1977 by Marjorie Hamilton

Ruth Hertzberg, Beatrice Vaughan and Janet Greene, *Putting Food By,* © 1973, 1974, 1975, 1982 by The Stephen Greene Press

Beverly Kees, *Basic Breads Around the World* © 1977 by Beverly Kees

Esther Munroe, *Sprouts to Grow and Eat,* © 1974 by Esther Munroe

Samuel R. Ogden, *Pan and Griddle Cakes,* © 1973 by Samuel R. Ogden

Julia Older and Steve Sherman, *Soup and Bread,* © 1978 by Julia Older and Steve Sherman

Denise Khaitman Schorr, *My French Kitchen,* © 1981 by Denise Khaitman Schorr

Jean H. Shepard, *The Harvest Home Steak Cookbook,* © 1973 by Jean H. Shepard

Camille J. Stagg, *The Cook's Advisor,* © 1982 by Camille J. Stagg

James Vilkitis and Susan Uhlinger, *Fish Cookery,* © 1974 by James R. Vilkitis and Susan J. Uhlinger

So many recipes were taken from the cookbooks of the prolific Beatrice Vaughan, that we list her cookbooks separately:

Citrus Cooking, © 1972 by Beatrice Vaughan
Jams, Jellies & Marmalades, © 1971 by Beatrice Vaughan
The Ladies Aid Cookbook, © 1971 by Beatrice Vaughan
The Old Cook's Almanac, © 1966 by Beatrice Vaughan
Pickles, Relishes & Preserves, © 1971 by Beatrice Vaughan
Real, Old-Time Yankee Apple Cooking, © 1969 by Beatrice Vaughan
Real, Old-Time Yankee Maple Cooking, © 1969 by Beatrice Vaughan
Store-Cheese Cooking, © 1968 by Beatrice Vaughan
Yankee Hill-Country Cooking, © 1963 by Beatrice Vaughan

All of the books listed above were published by The Stephen Greene Press, Fessenden Road, Brattleboro, Vermont 05301. We also gratefully acknowledge the kind permission which allowed us to include recipes from *The Natural World Cookbook—Complete Gourmet Meals from Wild Edibles* by Joe Freitus, © 1980 by Stone Wall Press, Inc.

Stone Wall Press, Inc. publishes *The Natural World Cookbook—Complete Gourmet Meals from Wild Edibles* by Joe Freitus (316 pages, illustrated, index, Hardcover $25.00). Available from Stackpole Books, Box 1831, Harrisburg, PA 17105.

Thanks also go to a most helpful typist, Elizabeth Kent.

Index